STITCH RHYTHMS & PATTERNS

JAN BEANEY & JEAN LITTLEJOHN

Contents

Introduction – All stitching is rhythmic

Sewing on a button, stitching a picture, beading a necklace or quilting a cushion illustrates this fact. Stitching requires a number of actions such as being worked under, over, through or around fibres on a background fabric or forming thread arrangements on a surface.

Machine stitching also calls for rhythmic movement where hand and eye co-ordination is necessary whether stitching decorative patterns or constructing a garment.

Design elements such as border patterns, repeating units and all sorts of printed imagery made with a sponge, a stencil or screen demand rhythmic actions to achieve certain effects. Negative and positive images, large and small scale and entwining or overlapping shapes encourage endless permutations of inventive pattern making.

The act of integrating designs may require rhythmic lines to suggest movement, to link and join elements or provide accents to unify or highlight.

Although the aim of this book is to concentrate on aspects of pattern making, many examples will contain practical, atmospheric, magical and possibly emotional content.

The rhythm of making a stitch is paramount. If time is spent really learning to look, there is much to be found in our environment to inspire wonderful stitch interpretations. We are surrounded by the regeneration of growth cycles within nature, seasonal changes, the very rhythm of life. Even introducing alien staccato or discordant rhythms to set up or arouse various moods and reactions could be considered.

In this book some words have been highlighted to illustrate the initial selection and development of thought processes and the choice of certain aspects of the design to be emphasised. In our previous books we have had the opportunities to explore a huge range of techniques and stitches and whilst we continue to use and adapt the most promising of innovations, we continue to develop and extend the potential of techniques that we have found most useful in the past.

We both love stitching and have enjoyed encrusting, layering and decorating its many types as appropriate to the look envisaged. Sometimes, intense beading or the use of the embellishing machine to blend or introduce a gentle dimensional affect have been selected. In many instances, some of the ideas could easily be adapted for a wide range of techniques.

The type of stitch plays a pivotal role in stitched textiles. There are times when they are used to link, coordinate and integrate work into the background, whereas on other occasions they can be massed together to form textures.

In this book we can highlight some 'diva' stitches and allow them to shine. The structures of the stitches, in some cases, have inspired samples.

Detached chain (lazy daisy) has the potential to be used for many purposes and in this book its structural and decorative properties have been fully exploited.

When criticised about decorative aspects of his work, Matisse is reported to have replied. "It's a bad mistake to give a pejorative sense of the word 'decorative'."

There are strategies for looking at familiar situations with fresh eyes and for looking for decorative and rhythmic elements in our daily lives as well as historical research to inspire us in new ways.

We hope that the joy of stitching and pattern making is evident and celebration is the order of the day.

Jan Beaney,   Jean Littlejohn

Gardens

Formal Gardens

Flowers displayed in formal gardens, window boxes and hanging baskets could suggest marvellous design starting points for many stitched projects. Many local parks, National Trust properties, stately homes, botanical and domestic gardens present symmetrical arrangements of a great variety of flowers and shrubs. Some celebrate unusual colour mixtures or are brazenly vivid, while others may be in a limited colour palette but with tonal variations.

The combinations of tall or low growing plants all with very different characteristics can suggest the stitch marks that can be used in embroidery. Some may be straight and stately, while others may show delicate fronds or clusters of tiny blooms.

The planting may be arranged in geometric patterns of triangles, diamonds, circles within circles or narrow and wide stripes both straight or curving. The choice can be endless. A row of window boxes or hanging baskets displayed in a gardening centre could suggest another approach.

Although the following illustrations show hand and machine stitched samples exploiting textural qualities, this source of design could be adjusted to suit other techniques. Many of the shapes in formal gardens could inspire ideas for canvas work, quilting and all forms of appliqué.

Location: Cliveden House, Berkshire, UK.

Flowerbeds planted between low hedges set out in a geometrical formation can be viewed from the rear of the big house and they always look most attractive. The multi coloured flowers contrasted beautifully with the grey green of the box hedging. The choice of plants and colours schemes change each year. The most recent visit revealed red geraniums placed to form diamond patterns repeated along the length of the bed with fading white flowers edging the basic shape.

The designs shown could be made larger or smaller in scale depending on the venture in mind. It may be suitable for projects such as beading, bonded surfaces, appliqué and canvas work. The latter may require the pattern to be transferred to graph paper in order to make the design more geometric and suitable for a counted thread technique. Layered stitches and beading could still be added if appropriate for the project in hand.

Key points: The triangular areas that edged the bed were filled with large, almost 'blousy', brightly coloured marigolds that were very dominant and this aspect was selected to be the main focus.

Design: A quick sketch accompanied by colour and textural notes was made. The pattern was simplified and painted with broad textual marks representing the general characteristics of the flowers without being too literal.

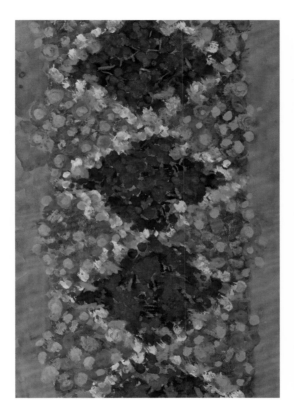

Techniques: The sample shown (see page 9) was such a joy to work, with the freedom to layer and decorate the stitches with a wonderful range of threads and beads. Layers of varied sized French knots and straight stitches were employed.

A second version of the design (see page 8) was worked in free motion machine and hand stitches on soluble film to create a delicate, lacy border. Looped and straight stitches, masses of beads and some sequins were used for this sample.

Location: Cliveden House, Long Garden, UK.

The general view was very impressive. The long straight lines of short, precisely clipped formal hedges enclosed large beds of clusters of pinkish, purple flowers. Simply shaped trees exhibiting lime green foliage added an accent to the vista.

Key points: Having made the decision to exaggerate the colour, the scene was simplified into bands of the chosen hues representing the flowers and hedges with the lime green tree shape introducing a rhythmic repeating device.

Design: Coloured papers were selected for the design process (see page 12). The collage could suggest a number of stitch interpretations.

Techniques: Tiny snippets of fabric and thread were bonded under a polyester 'chiffon' scarf on to a medium weight fabric to suggest the differing areas of the design (see page 13). Sorbello and a variety of straight stitches were worked in a range of silk and cotton yarns to decorate and texture this border pattern.

Size: Actual size.

The beaded sample shown opposite was inspired by the same garden but a square format was devised whereby the outside edge represented the hedges with the flowers set in the middle.

Techniques: Free motion machined lines were worked on 'Solusheet', an opaque soluble material ensuring that all sections were linked as shown in the diagrams.

Having machined a network of lines, tiny beads were stitched to them in the selected colour scheme before the dissolving process.

Size: Actual size.

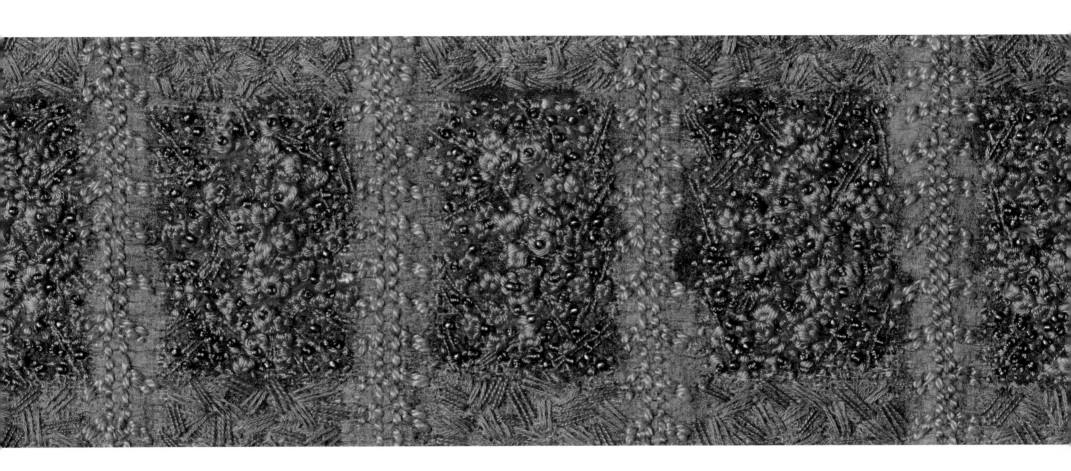

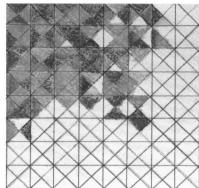

Grids from Gardens

Location: Rhododendron bushes, Kew Gardens, UK.

Key points: Kew Gardens are always a source of inspiration at any time of year but in the Spring the rhododendron bushes exude wonderful drifts of pinks, reds and orange flowers set against the green foliage.

Photographs or colour sketches can give an overall impression and act as a guide for a geometric or formal design.

The grid shown here was filled in with colours approximating to the proportions of the original drawing in preparation for the stylised stitch rendering of the idea.

Techniques: The stitched piece featured was worked on a dyed turquoise open weave cotton background to act as a contrast to the pinks and greens. Little glimpses of the ground colour show through to add a more dynamic element to the finished piece.

The whole sample was worked in detached chain (lazy daisy) stitch using a variety of fibres in a range of thicknesses from fine to chunky.

Size: H: 21cms/8¼inches
W: 30cms/12inches

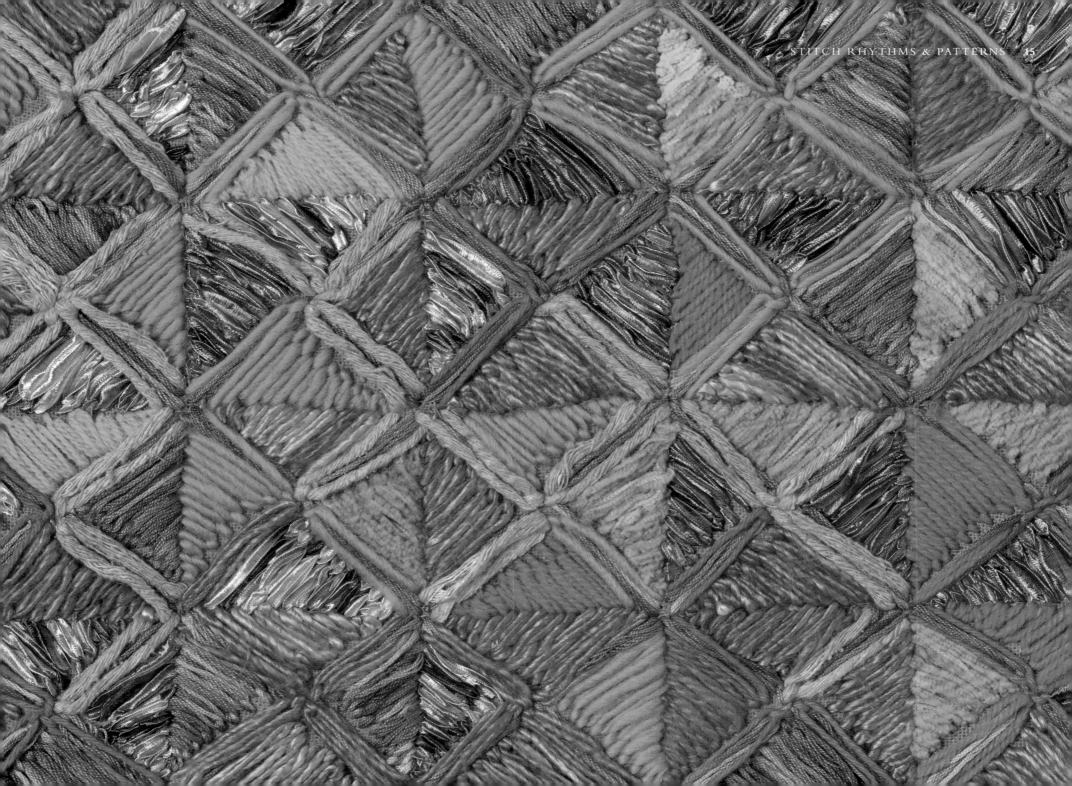

Spring Borders

Location: Kew Gardens, UK.

Key points: The Spring borders are often planted in formal patterns but as they grow they burst into profuse textures and the formality becomes lost in a froth of flower heads and foliage.

The original drawing inspired a torn paper collage that enabled the complex shapes to be broken down into simpler forms.

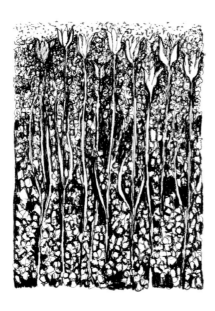

Techniques: The background comprises layers of fabric. The surface fabric is a discharge silk chiffon (prepared for colour removal) that has been printed with discharge paints to remove the colour and replace it with other colours. This was achieved by allowing it to dry before ironing with a steam iron (in a well ventilated space or outside) to get the dyes to work. (See Useful Information section page 93)

This is a fine, semi sheer fabric so bands of coloured lamé were placed underneath to shine through the chiffon and add further colour before stitching.

The simplified tulip, pansy and other shapes were bonded to the top surface before hand stitching. The prepared and bonded layers are shown to the left of the stitched piece.

Once the layers were complete they were put into a frame for hand stitching.

The stitches included looped French knots with sequins added, detached chain (lazy daisy), straight and seeding stitches and some additional beads to complete.

Size: H: 29cms/11½inches
W: 32cms/12½inches

Carpet of Flowers

Key points: Traditional Eastern carpets often feature flowers in formal arrangements and they can be an inspirational starting pint when looking at potential pattern sources to act as frameworks for ideas.

The two sketches show simple arrangements based on formal carpet borders that could be utilised in this way.

The final striped format was arrived at after developing ideas inspired by the Kew Garden designs from the previous page. The collage was photocopied and cut in various ways to explore ideas loosely based on the idea of striped patterned carpets.

Techniques: 'Aquabond' soluble fabric was used as a base to build up fibres and fabric scraps into free stripes of texture. The tulip shapes and stems were also applied in this way before the transparent layer of soluble support fabric was placed on top to form the fabric sandwich in preparation for the machine stitching. Once the machine stitching had been completed, the whole piece was dissolved in water and dried.

It was then cut into stripes and placed on a new piece of 'Aquabond' with spaces between the stripes.

Then a final piece of transparent soluble support was put over this arrangement, and further stitching worked to link the previously stitched stripes. When complete the whole piece was immersed in warm water to dissolve away all the soluble support fabrics before it was dried and stretched.

Size: H: 34cms/13½inches
W: 30cms/12inches

Cloth of Flowers

Location: The long garden at Cliveden provided yet another glorious vista to marvel at. Pink and red tulips were interspersed between clusters of tiny blue and purple flowers.

Key points: The bolder shapes of the larger blooms contrasted with the delicacy of the expanse of star shaped smaller ones. The attractive patterns suggested an idea for an all over design.

Aim: The aim was to create a lacy cloth where the blue and purple flowers would provide the main structure and allow the big blooms to feature.

Design: A quick colour sketch using coloured aquarelle crayons accompanied by photographs enabled the information to be used at a later date.

Techniques: An opaque, white soluble material such as 'Solusheet' or an equivilent was selected as it is easy to use and does not tear when machining delicate or intense areas of stitching. The simplified pattern was traced through using a sharpened pencil or ball point pen. The machine was set for free motion sewing and an appropriate darning foot fitted. Having stretched the cloth tautly in a frame, a green coloured machine thread was straight stitched meandering quite generally all over the material including going through the areas where the stylised tulips would be worked. This became the 'safety net' thus ensuring all areas were linked. This action was followed by stitching the tiny flowers in the chosen colour range making sure some of the lines linked with others and so continuing the process of building up the lacy network.

The larger flowers were filled in with lines of straight stitch to create stronger contrasting shapes. When machining solid shapes on soluble materials, it is useful to remember to stitch underpinning lines in the opposite direction to the intended top stitching making sure that they actually join the outside edge of the proposed area of design. This action will help to hold the shapes together during the dissolving process.

The cloth was plunged into several bowls of warm water to wash away the soluble ground cloth and rolled in a soft towel to remove excess water. It was stretched out and pinned onto a board and left to dry. This process is described in 'Stitchscapes' and 'In Action' DVD.

Size: Actual size.

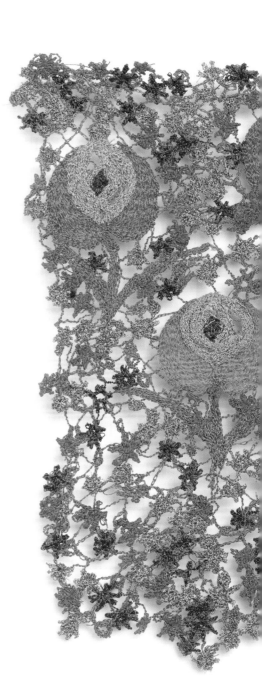

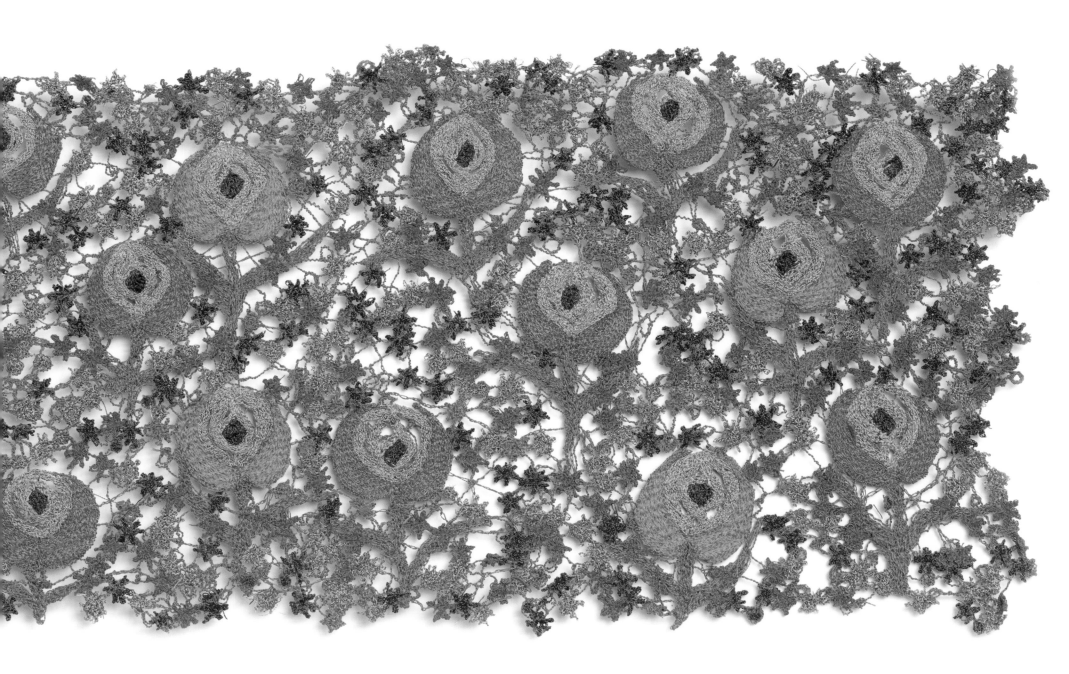

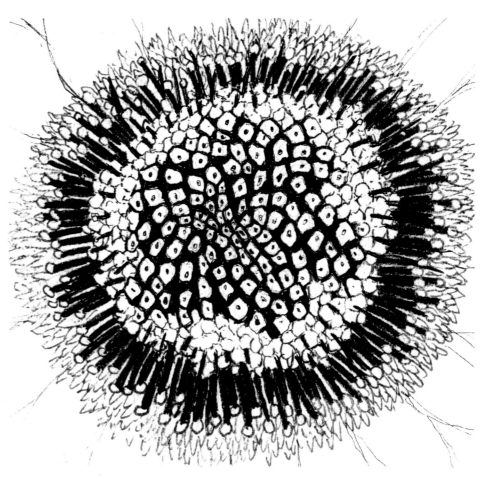

Flower Centres – A Closer Look

Centres of flowers burst forth in complex patterns to lure bees and other insects and thus ensure fertilisation and survival.

Key points: By isolating the centres, the colours and textures take on abstract and vibrant arrangements that give us amazing possibilities for design. There are exotic blooms such as dahlias, lilies and orchids that have obvious attractions but sometimes a seemingly humble flower like a daisy will have the most inspirational designs when examined under a magnifying glass.

Studies of centres such as the sunflower featured here can be painted or drawn to expose the structure and pattern and gain the information necessary for a stitched interpretation. The process of observation and drawing helps to simplify the image, a useful step towards a celebration of the source rather than a literal, photographic copy.

The aim of the stitched piece (right) was to explore the dimensional qualities of hand stitching and exploit the unique properties that stitched textiles offer.

Techniques: Hand stitching was worked on a light wool background which was held taut in a frame.

The structure of the sunflower centre was created with knotted cable chain and detached chain (lazy daisy). Woven picots stitched into the structure offered the little raised 'tongues' of texture interspersed with stitched tufts and loosely worked French knots. The final touches were added with beaded bugle beads standing proud of the surface.

Size: H: 21cms/8¼ inches
W: 21cms/8¼ inches

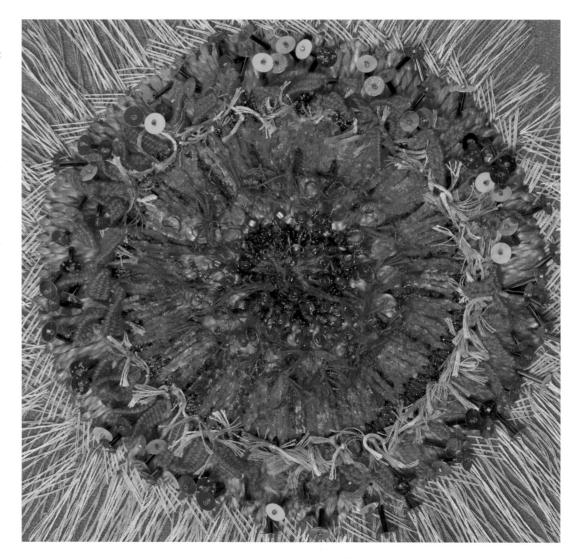

It has been a joy featuring flowers in this book and it could be inspirational and worthwhile to look even closer at more detail. By spending a little time observing the centres of flowers, many fascinating patterns can be discovered. Even more intriguing shapes will be revealed when magnified. Jot down the main characteristics taken out of context. These could be enlarged and placed in a variety of arrangements easily forming a basis of a design. The variety of stamens, stigma and sepals to be seen is quite outstanding.

The colours range from vivid hues to pastel shades and the textured surfaces exhibit all manner of star like protrusions, curly filaments and stiff bristles. These could be interpreted with layered stitches, wires, beads and other mixed media.

Some of these aspects can be partnered together to form attractive circular and border patterns for a range of projects.

The flower design shown opposite was initially inspired by a bottle brush flower. Some central areas were simplified and others exaggerated. The basic shape was cut from a fine net and bonded onto 'Solusheet', an opaque white soluble material. Long wool straight stitches were worked to form the green section. Machine stitching in a toning colour strengthened the area without totally flattening it.

The centre was filled with machine stitches before developing the textural areas. Machine stitched cords, looped stitches, long bugle and round beads decorated the middle with coloured wires and bugle beads splayed out of the centre encroaching and linking the outside edge.

Size: Actual size.

Cornucopia – An Abundance

Key points: There are innumerable historical sources involving floral patterns and the Victoria and Albert Museum is a wonderful source of inspiration. Time spent walking through the miles of galleries will repay itself in the richness of its inspirational items. From the complex repeat patterns of William Morris to the subtle simplicity of Japanese floral motifs, there is scope for a lifetime of study.

This piece celebrates the exuberance of decorative floral pieces from the Arts and Crafts period but given a fresh 'spin'.

Techniques: During the nineteenth century there was a tradition of embroidering onto a printed fabric to enrich it. An interesting exercise would be to find a floral cloth and embellish it but how much more interesting if you create the patterned fabric yourself to use as a background for improvising some dramatic rhythmic stitching.

The background pictured here was created by using a variety of printing and discharge (colour removal) techniques onto a black fabric prepared for discharge. (see left)

Traditional and self designed printing blocks and stencils were used to create a free interpretation of a decorative floral pattern.

Once printed the colour was discharged (removed) by ironing with a steam iron (outside and using a mask).

The resulting cloth then inspired some bonded applied shapes and free bold hand stitching.

French knots, straight and detached chain were the main stitches used.

Once the hand stitching had been completed machine embroidery was added by enhancing the shapes and using the semi formal patterns as a guide.

By working the hand stitching first a really bold and robust cloth with dimensional and tactile properties was achieved.

Finally beads and sequins were added to further evoke the spirit of 'Cornucopia'.

Size: H: 30cms/12inches
W: 49cms/19¼inches

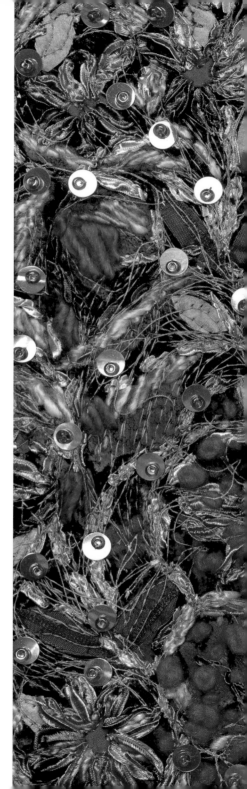

Patterns

The most humble objects and surfaces can be the jumping off point to many unusual or lively interpretations. Pathways, railings, fences, and barriers exhibit amazingly different variations of shapes and materials. When walking around your own locality many examples of these under valued surfaces can be observed, many of which you could easily pass by or walk over.

Patterns Under Foot

Location: Children's playground –
North London, UK.

Key points: The heavy duty rubber matting was placed beneath the swings and slides for the children's safety. The contrasting plain and textured surfaces of the tufts of grass growing through the symmetrically cut out pattern was appealing.

Design: A diagram was drawn of the basic structure using a black pen for boldness.

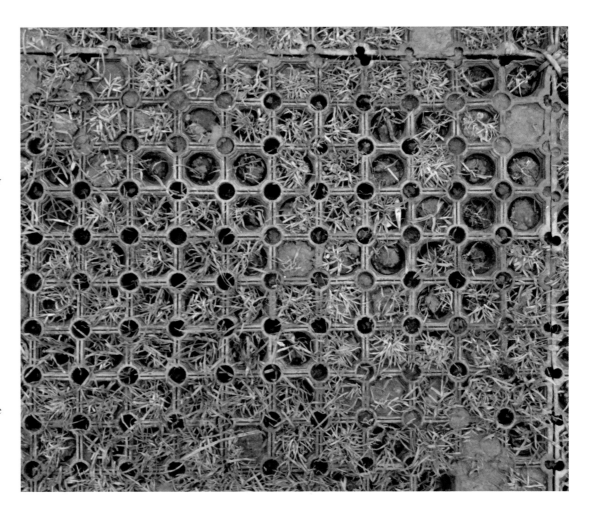

Techniques: The drawn pattern was placed under a piece of 'sticky' soluble material, 'Aquabond', which was taped to the work surface. A silk thread was placed on the sticky surface using the design beneath as a guide. A fine transparent soluble film, 'Guiliette', was placed on top. Straight machine stitch lines were worked through all the layers and over the thicker network beneath making sure that all sections were linked. A green metallic yarn was machined in a meandering manner to fill each of the central circular shapes. A randomly dyed thread was oversewn around most of the shapes. Cut looped threads, bugle and round beads were stitched in these areas to provide the contrasting texture that was the first attraction.

This type of approach could well inspire ideas for fashion accessories or textile jewellery.

Size: Actual size.

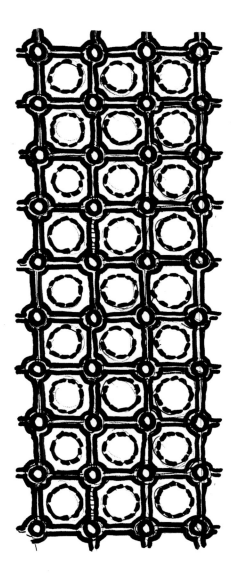

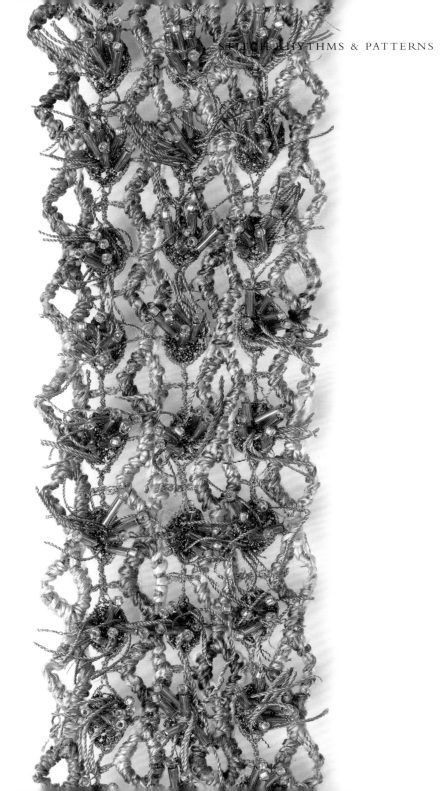

Repeating Units

Location: Skala Eressos, Lesbos, Greece.

These exotic flowers, discovered adorning several trees at this resort, were quite spectacular to observe and presented an intriguing challenge to draw. Following this close observation a simplified diagram was made which was almost symmetrical. This led to the process of cutting out several paper images in order to position them in a variety of arrangements. Those of you who prefer designing on the computer may feel happier to do that rather than the low 'tech' approach suggested.

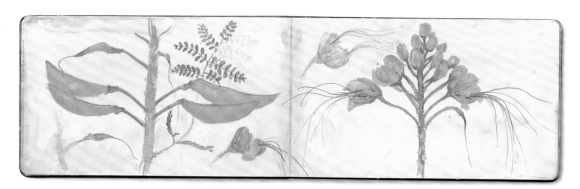

Techniques: In this instance a thermofax (see page 93) was made from the diagram. In trials, the motif was printed on several fabrics from sheer through to a synthetic velvet as the one illustrated opposite. Running stitches and French knots in silk yarns were used to develop the image further. This motif could easily be interpreted in machine embroidery, quilting or in appropriate stitching to decorate table linen.

Butterflies & Moths as Inspiration

Insects and in particular butterflies and moths have always been a great source of inspiration for artists and designers. If not carefully observed, the shapes of butterflies can be badly drawn and unsympathetically placed within a picture or design. These can result in heavy and clumsy renditions which completely lose the initial attraction of the characteristics of lightness and delicacy of these exquisite creatures.

However, patterns taken out of context may be more rewarding and fabulous designs can be developed. Butterflies exhibit unusual and subtle colours ranging from vivid hues and strong tonal contrasts to a gentle, soft shadowy and iridescent palette. There are many patterns to be seen within the wings and some motifs are reminiscent of eyes and are quite remarkable in their variations. The life like appearance may well ward off predators.

As suggested in previous publications, by jotting down the main proportions of the colours in your sketch or notebooks, new and innovative schemes could be used to give a fresh approach to a number of projects. If it is not possible to see live exhibits, many natural history museums house marvellous collections and the many books available could also help to give new ideas.

These intriguing insects could provide scope for developing interesting repeating units and numerous border patterns.

Locations: The Butterfly House, Callaway, Georgia, USA and a special summer exhibit at Kew Gardens, UK

The border pattern from the lower wings of the moth inspired the design illustrated.

Design: This was painted with gouache and metallic paints (see left).

Key points: The aim was to attempt to capture the subtle range of colours and markings as well as emphasising the delicate metallic qualities.

Techniques: The main lines of the design were freely drawn on the ground material with a coloured crayon. Stitched on a dyed, cotton fabric, Bokhara couching worked in silk threads was selected to develop the main areas of the design. Straight stitches, tiny French knots and beads were chosen to build up the textured section along with masses of delicate looped stitches in very fine metallic yarns (see right).

Size: H:23cms/9inches
W: 19cms/17½inches

Location: Kew Gardens, UK.

Key points: It had wonderful 'eye' motifs that exhibited unusual colours. This aspect appealed so a pattern was made of similar repeating motifs.

Design: the pattern was developed using 'Koh-I-Noor' dye based colour, aquarelle crayons and a little gouache to thicken the pigments in some areas.

Techniques: A black and white photocopy was made from the design and used to make a 'Thermofax' screen. This enabled several trials to be made by printing on a variety of materials. The range of screen printing inks and fabric paints now available are easy to use and leave very little residue or effect the feel of the cloth too much.

The image was printed on to a previously dyed cotton material (page 35, left). The transferred imagery provided a guide enabling the piece to be developed by working layers of straight stitches within the background areas. An embellishing machine was employed to very gently blend the thread work without felting it. Fine metallic and coloured yarns enriched the actual motifs.

Size: H: 21cms/8¼inches
W: 14cms/5½inches

The same motif inspired the decorative strip that could be developed further for jewellery and applied borders.

Sheer fabrics were placed on soluble film and machined stitched in place. Single stranded metallic threads in appropriate colours textured the surfaces with tiny beads to highlight.

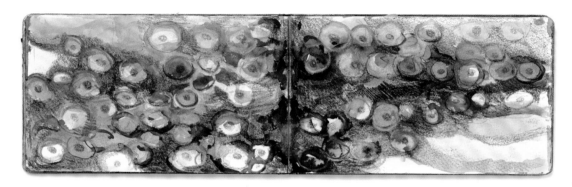

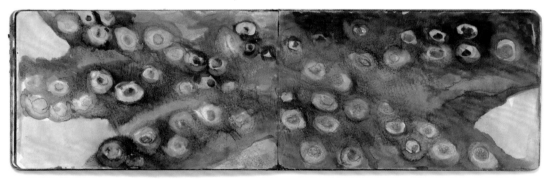

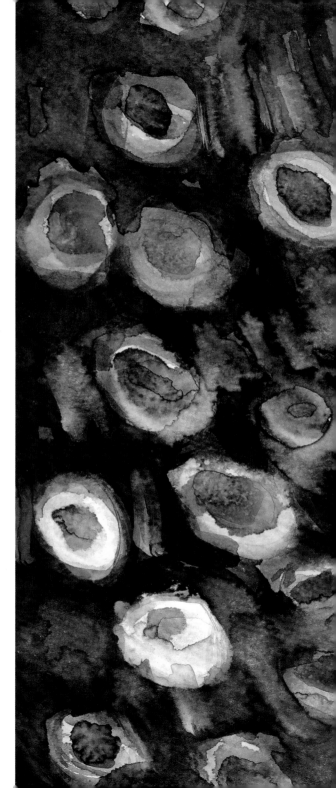

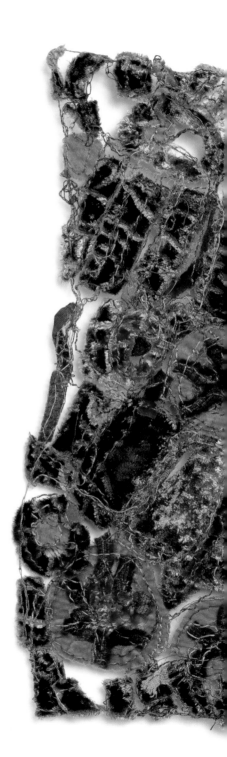

Spots & Stripes – Octopus

Key points: A holiday in Lesbos offered a wonderful opportunity to study an octopus very closely and the patterns and colours were amazingly varied. Original first hand studies were followed by more considered designs and each reworking of the image abstracted and stylised the patterns until spots and stripes became the dominant feature. These designs (pictured on previous pages) inspired the stitched interpretation seen here.

Techniques: This stylised octopus pattern has been worked on a water soluble ground. The detail (above) shows the sticky 'Aquabond' soluble backing, with the pattern shapes, cut from various velvets, stuck down and then sandwiched under a transparent sheet of non sticky water soluble 'Guiliette' ready for machining.

Useful guidelines when working in this medium include selecting a machine thread that is colour coordinated in order to link the elements in a harmonious way. If using a variegated thread ensure the colour contrasts are not too great as this can interfere with the overall effect. Be sure to link the shapes effectively and check by holding up to the light before dissolving the background in warm water. The weight of the velvet causes the fabric to hang really well.

Size: H: 25cms/10inches
W: 49cms/19¼inches

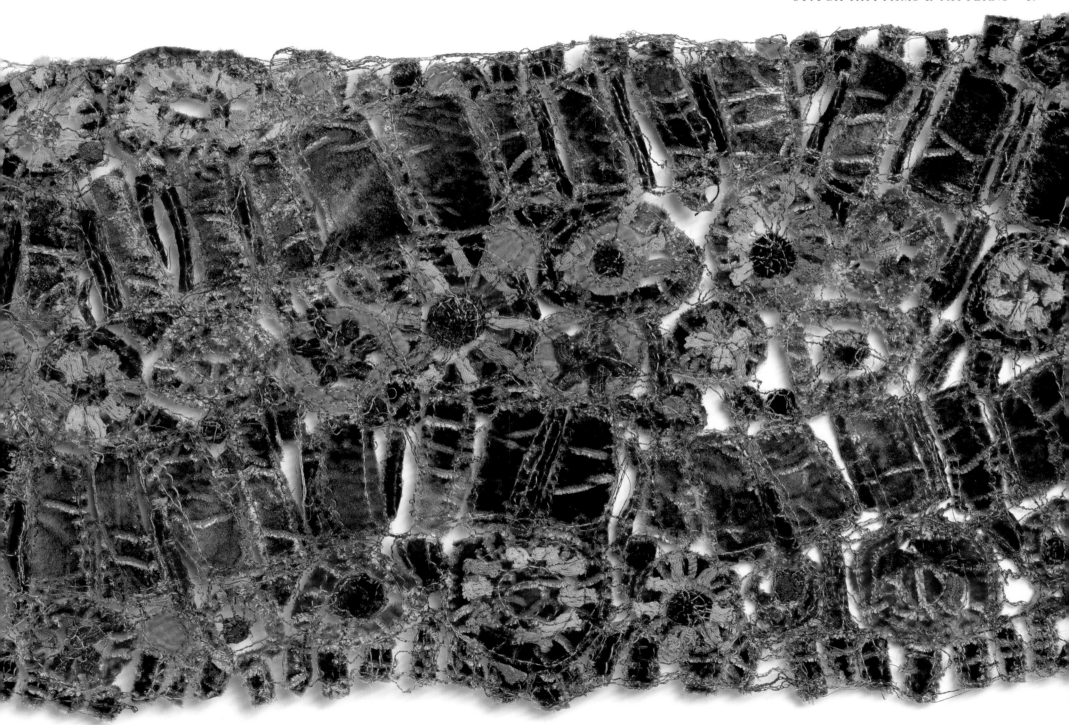

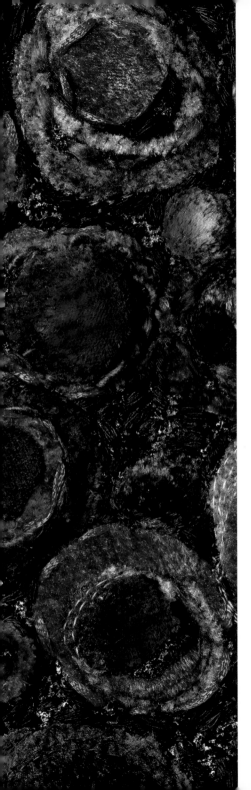

Circles & Spots – Log Piles

Location: St. Ulrich, Germany.

Key points: The patterns in a drying pile of logs looked good from a distance but on closer inspection the subtle colours of the differing annual rings in the drying wood were both surprising and inspirational. Several sketches and studies were made in order to exploit the circular shapes and exaggerate the colours into simplified designs.

Techniques: The background for the stitched piece featured here was fine purple wool.

Coloured synthetic velvets were selected for the circular shapes. These were first backed with 'Bondaweb' and then the circular shapes of varying sizes were drawn onto the supporting silicone paper. This backing makes it much easier to cut the shapes before removing the paper backing and ironing them onto the wool ground making a good textural contrast to the wool.

Once the applied shapes were completed the next stage was to echo and emphasize the circular structures

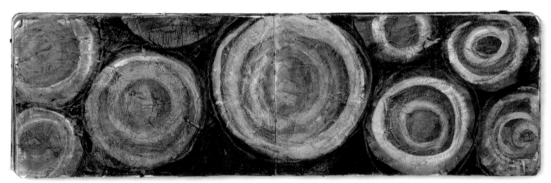

with bold hand stitching. This was mostly carried out in straight stitches and it is good to bear in mind that when working straight stitches in a fluid way, keep the spaces between the stitches small or they can look too staccato.

The final stage was to work machine stitches in order to integrate the different elements into the background and to cause the distortion that provided an extra dimensional quality.

Size: H: 21cms/8¼ inches
W: 74cms/29inches

Trees

Trees continually offer fabulous starting points for innovative designs. The flowers, seeds, fruits and leaves that they produce have featured in pattern making from ancient times. Due to age, climate and their immediate environment, colours are constantly changing and so offer continual inspiration.

The amazing bark surfaces to be found exhibit unusual colours, exciting textures and wonderful patterns. Linear, dimensional and repetitive rhythms could easily be an aspect to focus on.

Follow the Line

Location: Woodstock, New Jersey, USA.

Key points: When staying in a traditional house surrounded by broad leaf trees it was tempting to revisit this subject but with a fresh way of looking. The drawing illustrated here was made with a pen and the challenge was to record the information without removing the pen from the page once the drawing started. This may be a familiar exercise but it does cause very focussed observation and therefore a strategy that can be used many times to good effect. Before starting it is a good idea to identify the key rhythms and work out a logical pathway but during the working some unexpected moves have to be made and that often adds to the spontaneity of the image. In this way it is less likely to be tempted into a photographic interpretation. Another significant point is that a continuous line approach is helpful if machine embroidery is to be used.

Techniques: The stitched piece superimposed over the drawing has been constructed with a continuous line approach. The drawing was placed under a piece of 'Aquabond' taped to a flat surface. A continuous thread was placed on the major vertical and horizontal elements and a slightly finer thread used to represent the foliage. Care was taken to ensure that there were links between the different parts of the structure to ensure it would hold together when complete.

Transparent soluble support was then placed over the thread sandwich in preparation for machine stitching to reinforce the elements and add a finer dynamic to the piece.

It was then dissolved in warm water leaving a lace like piece inspired by the continuous line drawing.

Size: H: 26cms/10¼ inches
W: 32cms/12½ inches

Continuing the Line – Tea Tree Bark

Location: Tea Tree Lake, Byron Bay, Australia.

Key points: The lovely papery bark comprised compressed layers of fine linear fibres (see above).

Techniques: This piece of work, inspired by the bark, was constructed from layers of hand made dyed paper. Between each layer areas of couching were stitched to create some dimension to the piece.

The linear quality of hand couching seemed to be an obvious choice for completing the work along with some machine stitching for contrast.

Size: H: 21cms/8¼ inches
W: 52cms/20½ inches

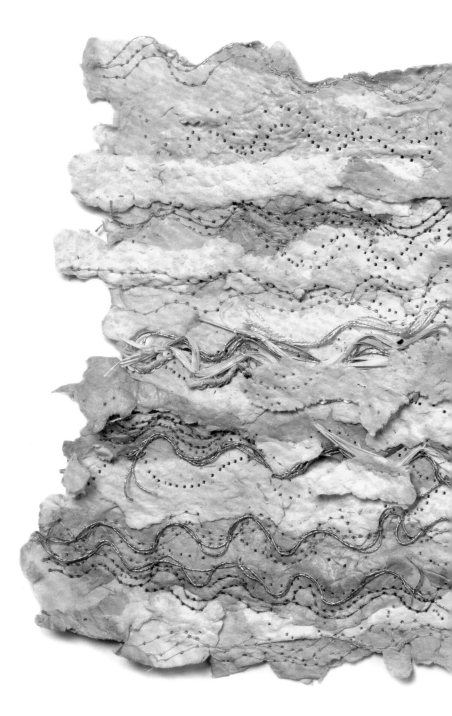

Distorting the Line – Palm bark

Location: Lismore, Australia.

Key points: The palm trees fringing the surf beach featured wonderful irregular linear patterns interspersed with spots and dots of texture. The colours were subtle hues of sandy yellows, greys and purples with a delicate silvery sheen.

Initial brief studies and photographs were followed by a more developed study (left).

Techniques: Knitting can be an excellent way of constructing a background for stitch and in this case when a linear structure was the underpinning rhythm, a range of fibres were knitted with careful attention being taken in selecting some really subtle colours.

When the knitting was complete the whole piece was placed under the needles of a needle punch (embellishing) machine to fuse and blend the colours, An embellishing machine is a marvellous way of 'bruising' and blending colours rather like smudging pastels in a drawing. The embellishing machine can also be used to make ridges for a dimensional effect.

The resulting cloth made a good base for hand stitching and the knobbly spots that featured on the bark were made with knotted cable chain, an excellent stitch for raised circular textures. This would also make a good base for machine embroidery but the finishing touch in this case was the embellishing machine, used to integrate the knotted cable chain into the background knitting.

Size: H: 81cms/31inches
W: 26cms/10¼inches

Techniques: The outline design was drawn on paper which was then placed (design side) against a window or on a light box in order to trace the design in reverse. The white side of a piece of 'Tap' paper (see page 93) was positioned on to the paper with the reversed design and using the same procedure as above, the outline drawing traced using a soft pencil so as not to damage the surface. Many people may choose to print a design from their computer onto this paper although the low-tech method has been explained in this instance. 'Koh-I-Noor' paints were then applied to build up the colour. When dried, the 'Tap' paper was placed painted side down onto a cotton fabric. Using a hot iron the design was transferred from the paper to the cloth. To develop the embroidered piece (far right), a variety of straight stitches were worked in cotton and linen yarns with a fine metallic silver thread to highlight.

Size: H:18cms/7inches
W:24cms/9½inches

Bark Rhythms

Location: Sedona, Arizona, USA.

Key points: These ancient trees, called Alligator Bark Junipers were observed while travelling off track on the higher ridges of the magnificent rock formations that surround Sedona. The subtle coloured bark was heavily textured and striking to observe and very reminiscent of the reptile after which it was named. The rhythmic placing of the deep cracks emphasised the raised layers of splitting wood strips.

Design: 'Koh-I-Noor' paints were used to block in the main areas of colour and black felt pen and white pencil were added to mark the dark crevices and the light dimensional surfaces.

Key points: To simplify the pattern and concentrate on emphasising the rhythmic lines of the deep fissures and the slightly raised elements so endeavouring to capture the essence of the surface without being too literal.

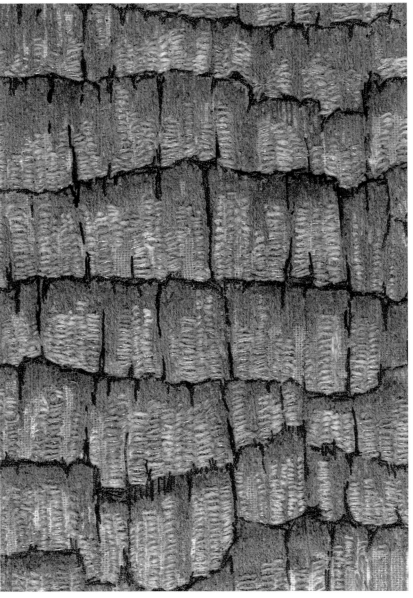

Winter Magic

Winter frost can transform gardens, trees, ponds and landscapes into beautiful atmospheric scenes of soft, muted colours. Even more stunning can be the more unusual 'hoar' frost that occasionally happens each winter. It clads all surfaces with dramatic, long spikes of frozen water. Not only does it change all the familiar characteristics of everyday surroundings, it also adds a jewel-like sparkle which is quite magical. Frost covered stems, leaves, grasses, lichen and water are just some that display fascinating textures for perhaps just a few hours or one day.

Frost patterns on windows could inspire a number of textile treatments from beaded cords to machine stitched lace. Jewellery, lacy curtains or close up interpretations of crystal 'collared' lichen or silvered leaves could present fascinating challenges.

Location: An English Garden, UK.

Key points: The aim was to try and capture the frosty qualities in a simple arrangement of leaves.

Techniques: Leaf shapes were cut from a firm fabric and positioned on a sticky soluble material. Once the design was built up, a transparent soluble film was placed on top to 'sandwich' all pieces firmly in place. Silver metallic machine thread was machined to edge each leaf in a spiky manner as well as joining all the elements together to form a linking network. Lots of tiny, clear beads were sewn on all parts to texture the surface. This process was completed before dissolving the stabilisers away. Glitter paint was applied sparingly onto the leaves for an extra glint.

Diagonal Rhythms

Location: Masseria della Zingara, Puglia, Italy.

This rugged, ancient tree was so noticeable standing in isolation within a large open space near the farmhouse. On closer inspection, the diagonal ridges and crevices were covered in mustard and orange lichen which showed up so brightly in the late autumn sunshine.

Key points: The glowing colour and the diagonal rhythms of the contours of the bark were the main factors to highlight.

Design: The sketch shown was drawn with coloured pencils and aquarelle crayons.

Techniques: Small pieces of scrim, wool tops and silk waste were placed on the sticky soluble material, 'Washaway Adhesive' or 'Aquabond'. When the main part of the design was built up, transparent soluble film was placed on top. Free motion machine stitching was meandered all over the piece ensuring that the lines resembled the characteristics of the textures observed as well as supplying the linking mechanism to hold the whole piece together. The aim was to capture the overall feeling of the surfaces without being too literal. Knotted stitches, wrapping and straight stitches were used to exaggerate and develop the layers of the lichen clad bark.

Size: Actual size.

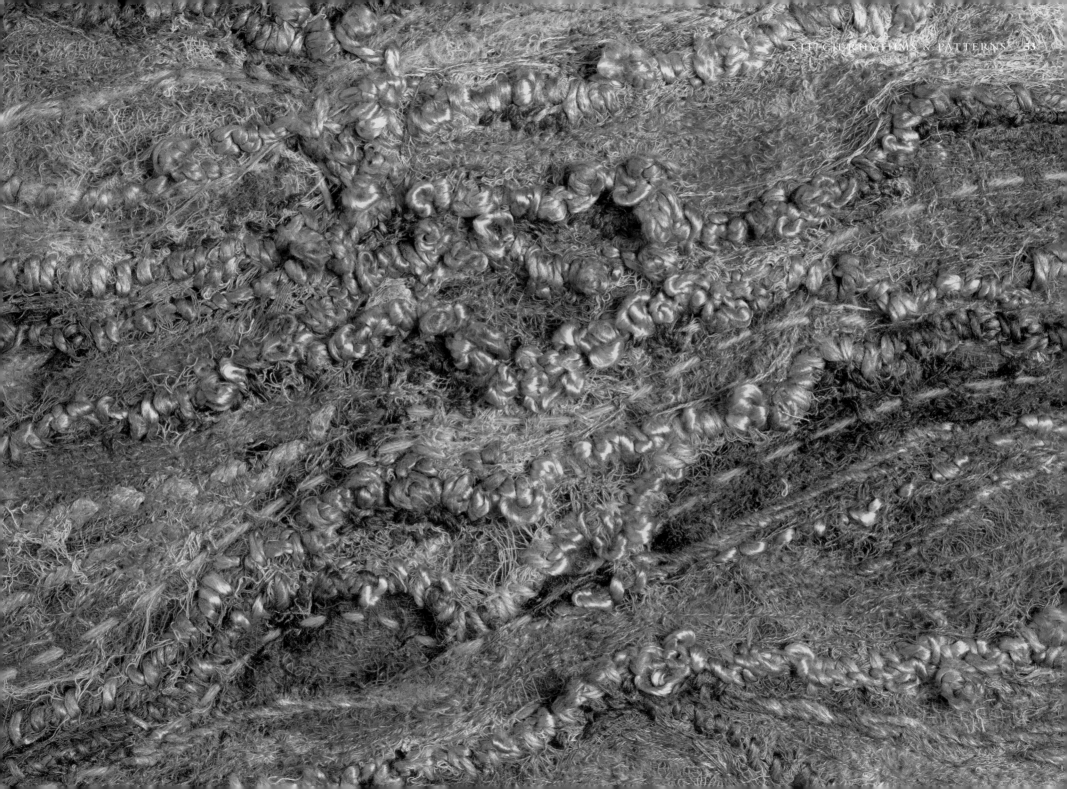

Forest Glade

Location: Pine forest, Blackberry Bog, Canada.

Key points: An opening in the pine woods threw light on the fringes of the branches producing dancing drifts of subtle colours.

The drawing featured (left) was the inspiration for the stitched piece shown (above). The drawing was worked with 'Koh-I-Noor' colours and aquarelle crayons on watercolour paper.

Techniques: The stitched sample was worked entirely in fly stitch.

Instead of worrying about the selection of the appropriate stitch, all concentration can be focussed on exploiting the structure, scale and direction of the selected stitch in order to interpret the design.

The stitches can also be overlapped, piled up and distorted to achieve the desired effect.

The resulting piece reflects the original idea but creates a stylised version.

Size: H: 12cms/4¾inches
W: 24cms/9½inches

Water

Undersea Rhythms

Location: Skala Erressos, Lesbos, Greece.

Key points: An underwater camera was used to record the encrusted rock formations close to the shore on this lovely Greek beach. Drawings and designs were then worked to explore the design possibilities. (see below) At first sight the underwater terrain looks textural and complex but on closer inspection the patterns can be broken down into simple groups of organisms that hug the rocks. The ebb and flow of the tides cause the formation of simple rhythms in the ripples on the sand and affect the way in which things grow. The underlying spiral form is a universal element in so many natural forms and features as the repeating element in this piece of work.

Techniques: A dyed heavy silk ground formed the base for this piece and painted 'Bondaweb' was ironed over the surface. (The 'Bondaweb' was

painted with acrylic and iridescent paints to create a sheen). This had the effect of adding colour and pattern and the surface could be reactivated with heat to remain sticky.

The next stage was to iron over an iridescent printing foil using silicone paper to protect the work and an iron set at no hotter than wool heat. This acted as a base for the placement of fibres, threads and some chopped and frayed fabrics.

Once the fibres had been organized a sheer polyester scarf was placed on top (protected by silicone parchment) and ironed over to trap the 'fabric sandwich'.

The piece was further enriched with hand stitching, including French knots and straight stitches and some iridescent sequins and beads.

Size: H: 22cms/8¾inches
W: 40cms/16inches

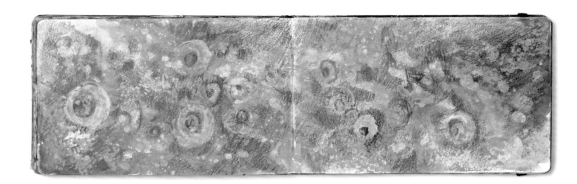

Mary's Pool

Location: The swimming pool of Mary, a friend in Sedona, USA.

Key points: Sedona is a marvellous and inspiring place surrounded by monumental rock formations, but sometimes the inspiration can come from something much more intimate than the epic scenery and a serene infinity pool was a wonderful source of colour and pattern.

The glass mosaic tiles were subtle greys, pinks and blues and in early morning and late evening the shadows on the surface were most amazing and reflected and distorted the architecture and scenery in a most inspiring way, changing second by second.

Sketchbook studies with photographic backup provided information for many pieces of work.

Some photographs were taken by crouching in the water and looking along the ripples on the surface.

The piece, 'Evening Tiles', seen opposite shows a stitched study of the glass tiles surrounding the pool.

Techniques: Squares of painted 'Bondaweb' were bonded onto a cotton ground fabric and silver foil ironed over the top to pick up the square shapes and leave the background spaces plain (see right). A sheer polyester scarf sealed the work ready for stitching.

After stretching the fabric into a frame for hand stitching the piece was stitched using Romanian couching and couched antique bugle beads.

Size: H: 16cms/6½ inches
W: 25cms/9¾ inches

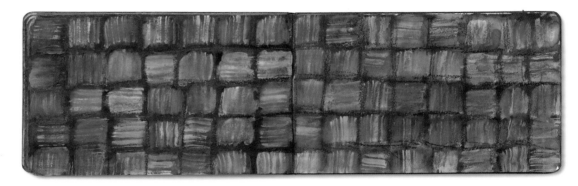

Surface studies
of the pool taken
at different times
of day.

Far right three
sketchbook
studies using
'Koh-I-Noor'
and aquarelle
crayons.

The other studies
were worked on
water colour
paper using
'Koh-I-Noor'
and aquarelle
crayons.

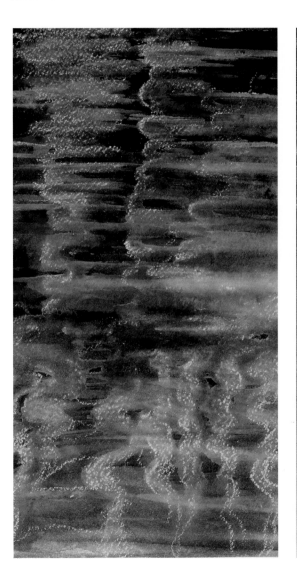

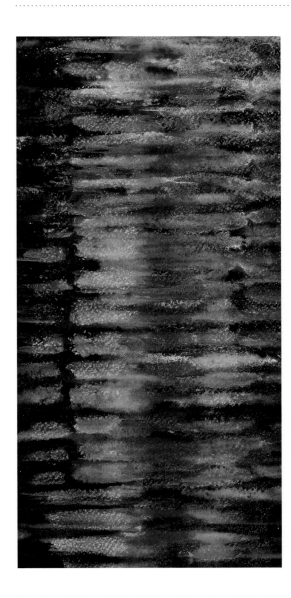

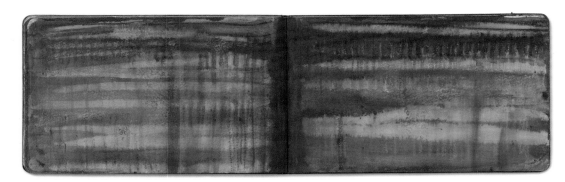

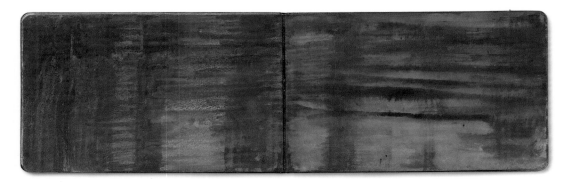

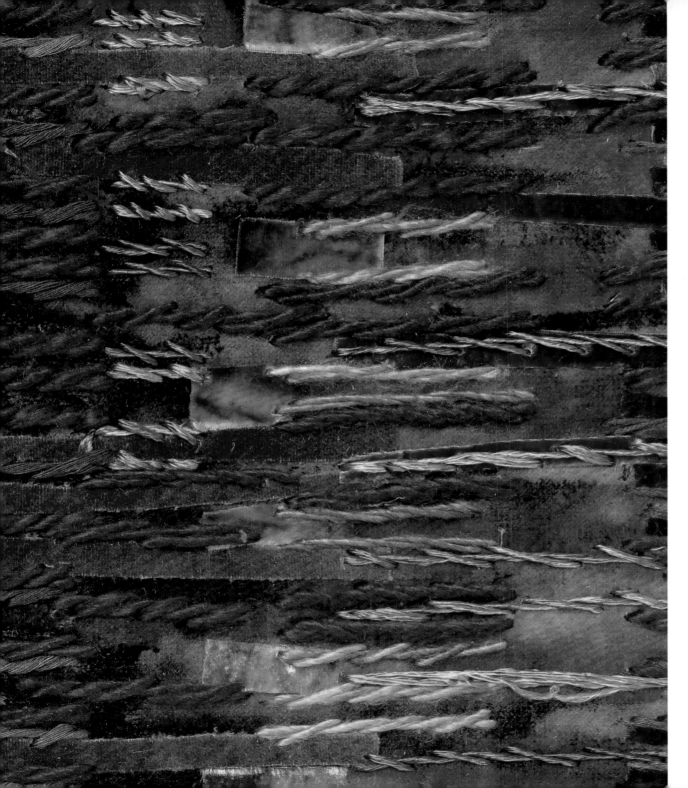

Techniques: Inspired by the studies on the previous pages this piece, 'Sunset Ripples', has been created by using discharge dyes, 'deColourant Plus', on a prepared ground to remove the dark colour and replace it with ripples of colour during the ironing process.

Simple shapes were bonded on to reinforce the linear rhythms and the hand stitching was carried out using only Romanian couching.

Size: H: 30cms/12inches
W: 60cms/24inches

Patterns Beneath

Water patterns and their ever changing colour combinations continually surprise, intrigue and present exciting possibilities. However drawing or painting the sea is always challenging. It is difficult to capture the essence of the colours as they are forever changing due to the reflections of the sky above and the continual motion of the water.

Waves, spewing foam, rhythmic or star shaped reflections, seaweed, stones or sand ripples on the sea bed can all offer fabulous ideas for making patterns.

Location: Tunisia.

Key points: The sea was very shallow and the swaying tufts of seaweed most surprisingly appeared to grow in quite organised diagonal patterns. Sand ripples added another element along with reflections from the sun.

Aim: So as not to complicate the design, the turquoise and green colours of the sea and the diagonal growth of the seaweed was selected for emphasis while the other aspects were ignored or understated.

Techniques: The design was applied onto paper using Transfer or Disperse dyes. Remember to paint the image in reverse if it must be viewed in a particular way. In general, this may not apply when pattern making. When dry, the image was transferred by iron from the paper to a synthetic fabric that resulted in a very brightly coloured image. For ease of working and to bear the weight of the stitching, the light weight, shiny material was backed by a soft calico fabric before starting. Using the colour of the print as inspiration, the surface was developed by machining blocks of straight stitches in blue and green coloured cotton threads blending one in to another. Hand stitching and beading depicted the seaweed and star shaped reflections.

Size: H:19cms/7½inches
W: 24cms/9½inches

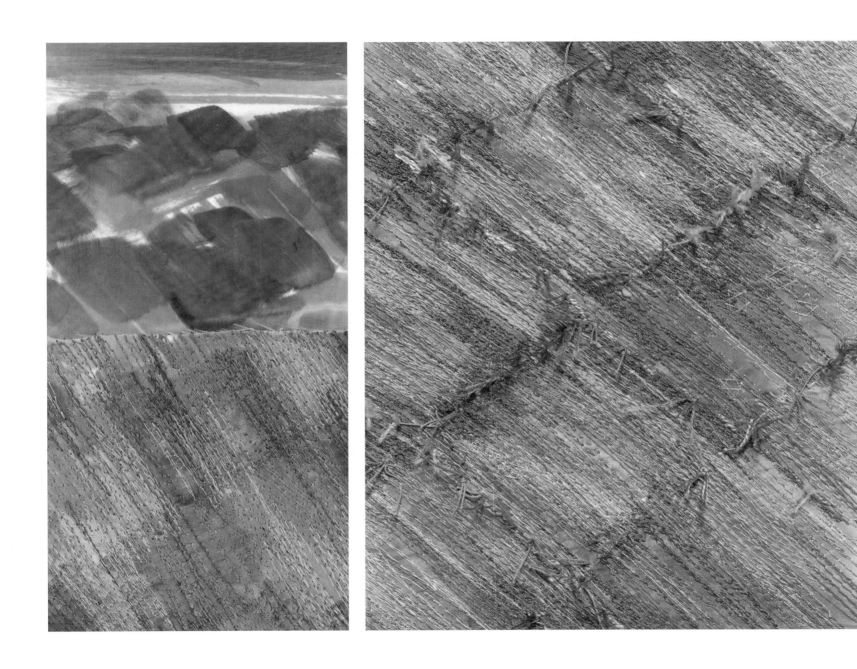

Landscapes

Stylisation – Simplification

Location: Masseria della Zingara, Puglia, Italy.

This is a beautifully restored farmhouse set within fields of fruit trees and with an abundance of wild flowers.

The visits made have been near the end of the summer when the trees have lost most of their leaves thus exposing more clearly the structures and shapes of the branches.

Several ideas were developed using the information collected. Elements were selected or combined where certain features were fitted within a striped arrangement of the original views.

Design: The sketchbook drawings were made using pencils, aquarelle crayons and various paints.

As illustrated opposite, simple line drawings and copies were made in order to experiment with various arrangements before embarking on any embroidered trials. Collage is another method of simplifying the imagery (far right).

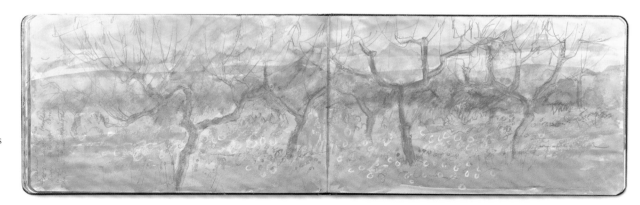

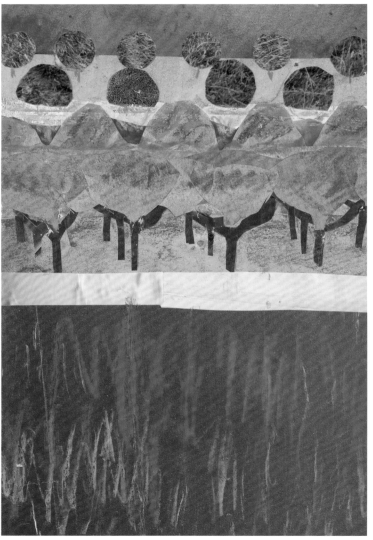

Aim: The aim was to experiment with screen printing to make a variety of a simple repeating patterned units that could be suitable for cushions or quilts.

Techniques: A group of trees with similar shapes as the ones sketched was reworked as a simple line drawing that was then transferred onto a 'thermofax' screen. Using an appropriate fabric paint, the images were printed onto a firm cotton fabric several times to form a repeating border pattern. When dry, the imagery was ironed to fix. The fabric was then dampened so that watered down silk paints when applied would blend one to another without leaving hard lines. The same procedure as above was followed to set the colour.

Fabric was prepared for quilting by tacking it on top of wadding/batting along with a soft calico backing cloth to make a 'sandwich' of three layers.

This partially worked piece, page 69, shows that a medium weight weaving yarn was backstitched along the lines of the design and French knots with loops spot quilted other sections suggesting the foliage between the trees.

Size: H: 28cms/11 inches
W: 30cms/12 inches

Another interpretation inspired again by Puglia on pages 70-71 exploited the interesting shapes of the trees to be seen in the surrounding countryside.

Aim: The aim was to use them as the main linking element within the lacy network. It was also meant to celebrate all the attractive aspects witnessed over many visits.

Simplified distant views, drifts of tiny marigold flowers, delicate white blooms and grasses were to be incorporated within the border.

Techniques: Threads, ribbons and small pieces of scrim were positioned on a sticky soluble material to establish the top and lower horizontal lines. 'Guiliette', a clear soluble film was placed on top to fix everything in place. The tree shapes were drawn on top with a spirit pen. Layers of back stitch were worked to fill these shapes in the first instance followed by machine stitching and a little blending with an embellishing machine. All other areas were hand and machined stitched ensuring that all elements were linked both horizontally and vertically to form a totally new fabric after the soluble film was washed away.

Size: H: 70cms / 27½ inches
W: 18cms / 7 inches

Aim: To make a small picture that captured the characteristics of the location by stylising and simplifying the main aspects to form a flat pattern.

Techniques: Some small pieces of fabric were bonded onto a fine wool ground fabric to suggest the main areas of colour. Surface stitches including couching, straight and seeding stitches were used throughout. French knots decorated the arched treetops.

Size: H: 16cms/ 6½inches W: 24cms/ 9½inches

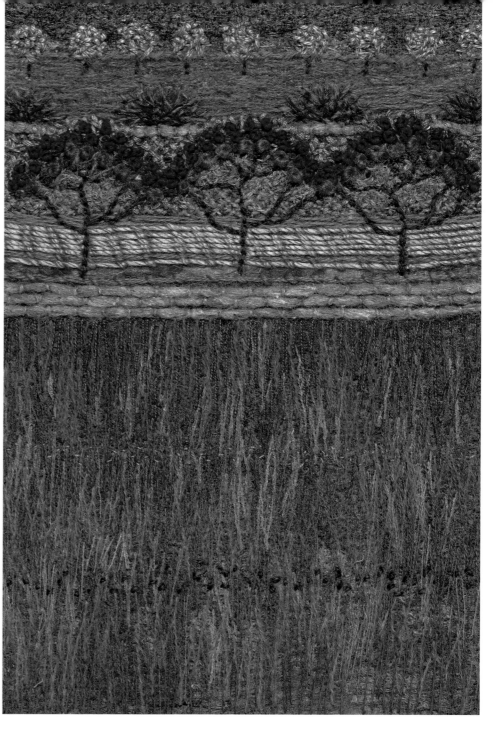

Sedona Landscape

If rhythms and patterns are the main focus, these can be found within many landscapes. This particular area near Sedona was spectacular. In many cases, the red rock contrasted with the green, grey vegetation which in certain lights looked quite turquoise in colour. A fascinating feature was the diagonal growth patterns at the base of many of the ridges. Some appeared so manicured that it almost looked as if man had interfered with the formation.

Key points: The colour, diagonal and horizontal lines were the main consideration when planning the design.

Design: The sketches were drawn with 'Koh-I-Noor' colours, pencil and aquarelle crayons.

Techniques: A dyed purple coloured cotton cloth was selected for the background. Colour was added by applying 'deColourant Plus' which is a product that removes the base colour but adds a new one. The border strip was painted using this method. When dry, ironing the surface completed the process of building up the colour. This all in one method seems to work well although always trial a range of fabrics before embarking on a project.

The surface was decorated with straight stitches in a variety of toning threads (see page 74–75).

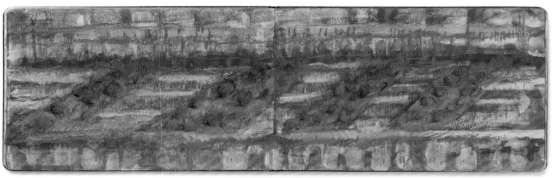

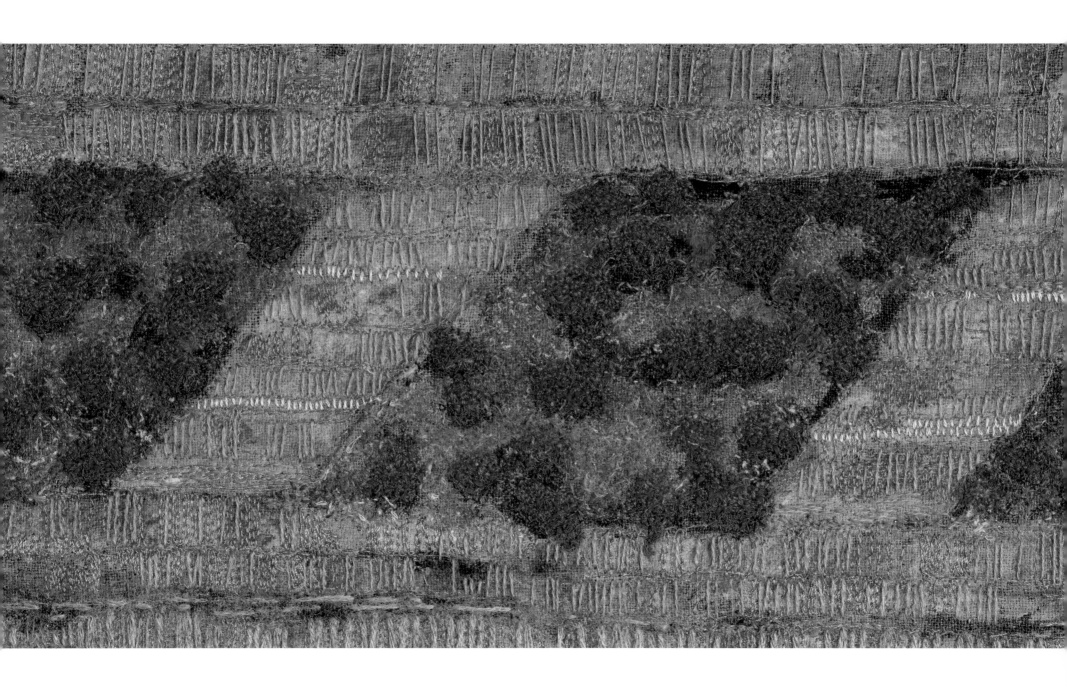

Rock Rhythms – Santa Fe

Location: Rock formations of Santa Fe, New Mexico, USA.

Key points: This sample (far right) reflects not just the landscape but also traditional Pueblo patterns from the local indigenous peoples. It was designed to explore the notion of man and his impact on landscape by combining the natural strata of the rocks with marks from ancient pots excavated from local sites.

The sketchbook pages show observations from both these sources with an initial design idea for the sample.

Techniques: Cotton scrim was dyed and over dyed on a heavily creased and crumpled fabric to encourage an uneven taking up of the dyes to echo the strata of the landscape.

An area was selected from the fabric and applied to a piece of dyed orange/ginger felt.

The two layers were then gently fused together with an embellishing machine to form the background cloth (see near right)

The hand stitching was based on the Pueblo patterns from the research and the colours selected to integrate them into the landscape without overpowering it and symbolise a harmony between man and his environment.

When the hand stitching was complete further embellishing was worked on the front and back of the fabric to further blend it with the ground.

Size: H: 30cms/12inches
W: 26cms/10¼inches

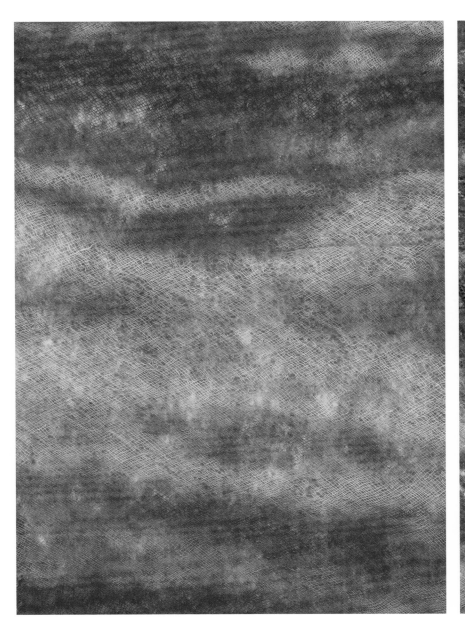

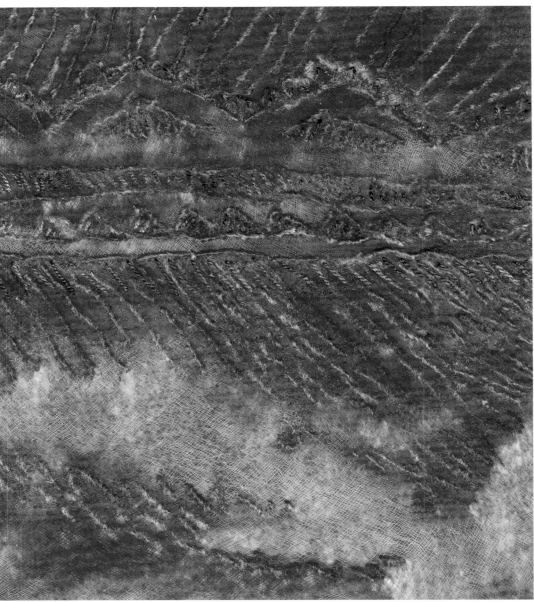

New Patterns, Familiar Sources

Location: Jean's house.

Key points: Redecorating and extending a Victorian building was a disruptive enterprise but the process exposed layers of pattern and colours from previous generations. This led to drawings and research around the idea of exploring patterns on this theme in preparation for fresh work. It takes time when beginning a new series and the first stage is to draw and explore design ideas.
It is best to try and keep an open mind to avoid repeating well worn familiar design paths.

The sketchbook pictured is an interesting format and comprises a continuous strip folded into a zigzag book. New design challenges can encourage different ways of thinking.
The pages were first painted in the colours of exposed plaster from the building work and various

printing blocks, stencils, templates and other relevant images were layered, printed, overlapped etc. to explore the ideas in a non-structured random way hoping that from this starting point ideas would emerge. This is an on going project and overdrawing or printing can be carried out as other ideas occur.

This format encouraged a freer approach and sections selected out of context formed the basis of the samples worked on the following pages.

Key points: The detail shown (below) has been extracted from the sketchbook featured on the previous pages. The elements in the design show aspects of pattern and texture from the building works combined with historical details.

Techniques: In 'Looking Back 1' lace and velvet shapes were bonded to a woollen background and then machine stitched.

Over this surface a layer of painted 'Bondaweb' was ironed to partially obscure the pattern. A sheer polyester scarf ironed over the 'Bondaweb' secured it ready for further work.

The idea of this piece was to make a pattern, obscure it and then retrieve it, thus echoing the sense of layers of history. An embellishing machine was used on the surface of the piece to integrate the elements and expose some of the pattern. The reverse side was also embellished to push some of the colour through to the front and further promoted the idea of merging layers. This machine is a marvellous way of fusing imagery and integrating and blurring layers of fabric.

When the preparation was complete hand and machine stitching completed the image.

Size: H: 37cms/14¼ inches
W: 41cms/16¼ inches

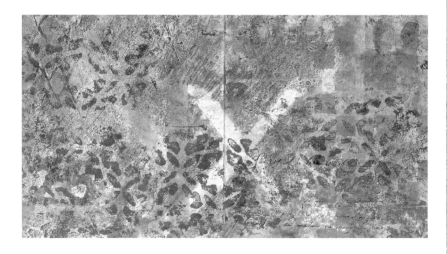

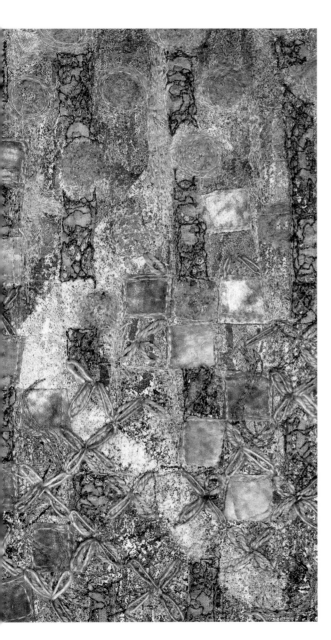

Techniques: The second sample, 'Looking Back 2', in this series was worked on natural coloured cotton scrim.

The bonded applied shapes were silk viscose undyed velvet.

The reason for using undyed materials was to allow the colours to be applied at a later stage and to this end it is important to remember to use cotton thread as polyester will resist the dyeing process.

Once the shapes were applied to the scrim the whole piece was stretched really taut in a frame prepared for machine embroidery. The white cotton thread on the bobbin and in the needle was machined into the image using free machine embroidery set on zigzag. The process distorts the scrim to pull it into interesting holes and spaces that echo and enhance the applied pattern. The shapes were secured with straight stitching.

When all the stitching was complete the whole piece was pinned out onto a corkboard with paper towel underneath.

Before colouring with acrylic fabric paints the cloth was sprayed with a mist of water so that the colours would more easily be absorbed and flow in an organic way. The colours tend to dry lighter so a second application may be necessary. In which case remember to spray it with water first to achieve a better result.

Size: H: 33cms/13inches
W: 24cms/9½inches

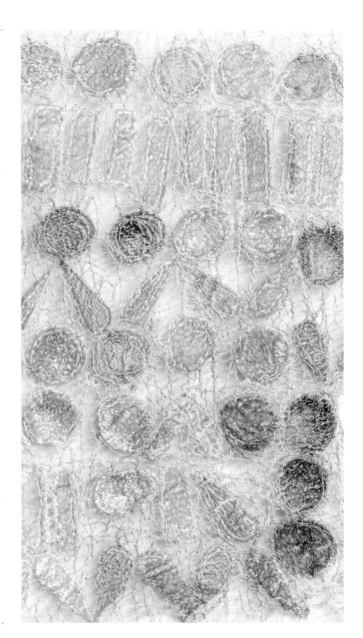

Key points: The main structure for this piece is also taken from the zigzag sketchbook on pages 78-79 but other elements have been added to further the idea of the past and present mix. The colours have also been influenced by fragments unearthed from the building works. The dark green and dull pink reflect the ethos of the Edwardian period.

Techniques: Bonded applied shapes on a wool ground form the basis of this piece, 'Then and Now', which was then embellished with the needle punch machine to integrate and blend the images into the background, To this, motifs cut from period brocade were stitched to the ground. By working from the reverse side the patterns were further blurred to reinforce the feeling of history. Machine and hand embroidery, reflected and echoed the patterns to complete the work.

Size: H: 37cms/14½inches
W: 41cms/16¼inches

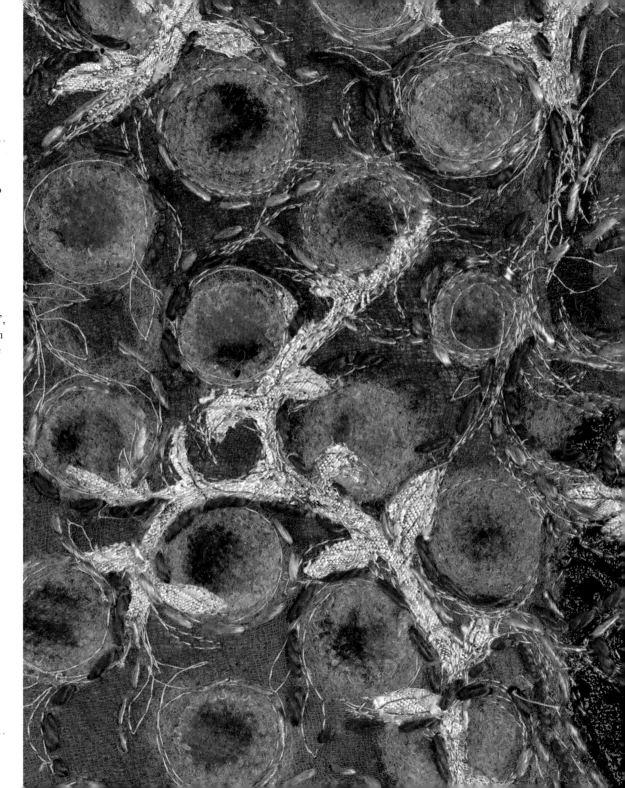

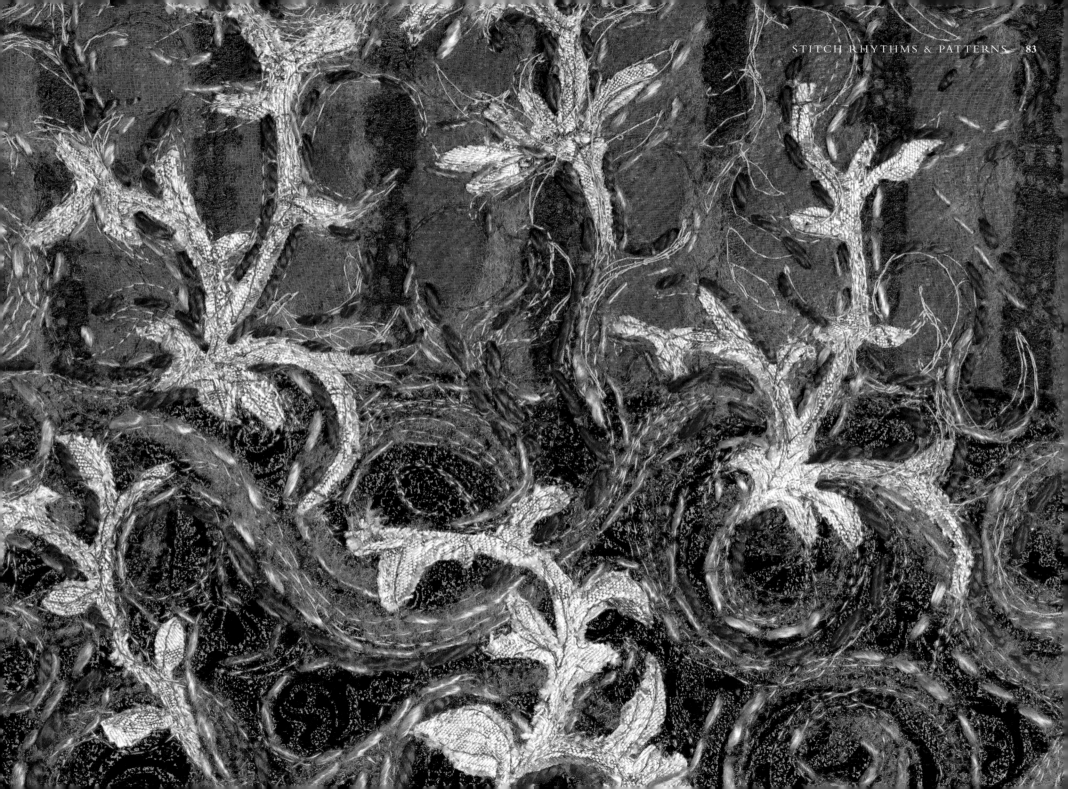

Stitch Diagrams

Stitches may be used in countless ways but it is when pattern is required that they can reveal their full structural potential.

Sometimes it is a question of finding the right stitch for a specific pattern but at other times the very pattern of the stitch can be the driving force behind a particular piece of work as illustrated in this book.

They can be butted up, overlapped, layered, beaded, whipped and embellished in numerous ways. The size of the stitch and the quality and thickness of thread may also be exploited to give endless variations.

There are many stitches that may be used but featured here are some of the stitches we have found particularly useful.

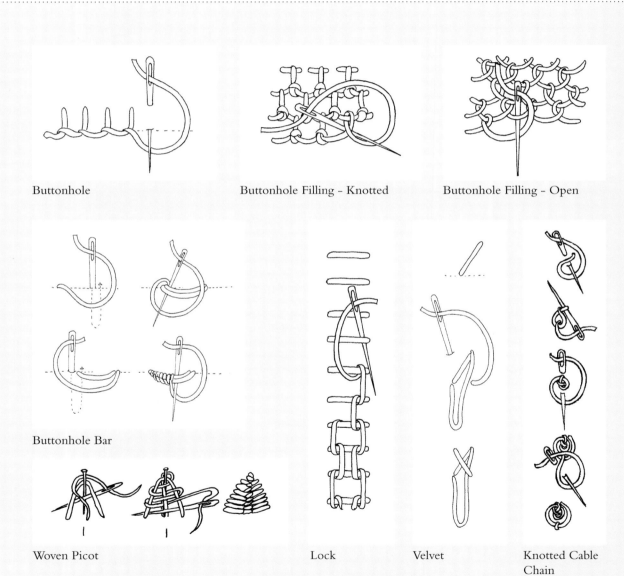

Buttonhole

Buttonhole Filling – Knotted

Buttonhole Filling – Open

Buttonhole Bar

Woven Picot

Lock

Velvet

Knotted Cable Chain

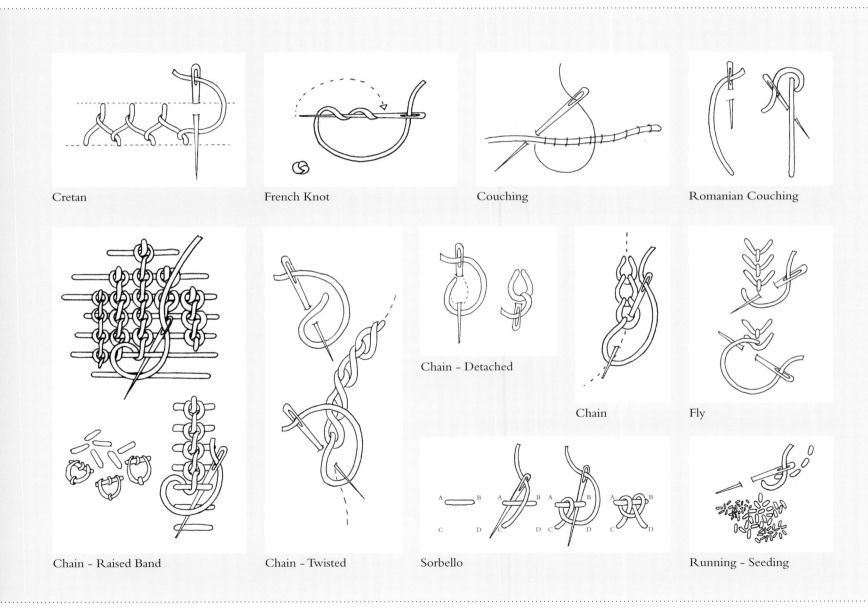

Cretan

French Knot

Couching

Romanian Couching

Chain – Raised Band

Chain – Twisted

Chain – Detached

Sorbello

Chain

Fly

Running – Seeding

Stitch Samples

1. Vertical and horizontal overlapping rows of lock stitch.

2. Vertical rows of lock stitch with isolated lock stitch centres.

3. Horizontal rows of upright fly stitch.

4. Horizontal rows of fly stitch worked on its side.

5. Knotted cable chain with contrasting twisted chain inserts.

6. Horizontal rows of wrapped knotted cable chain.

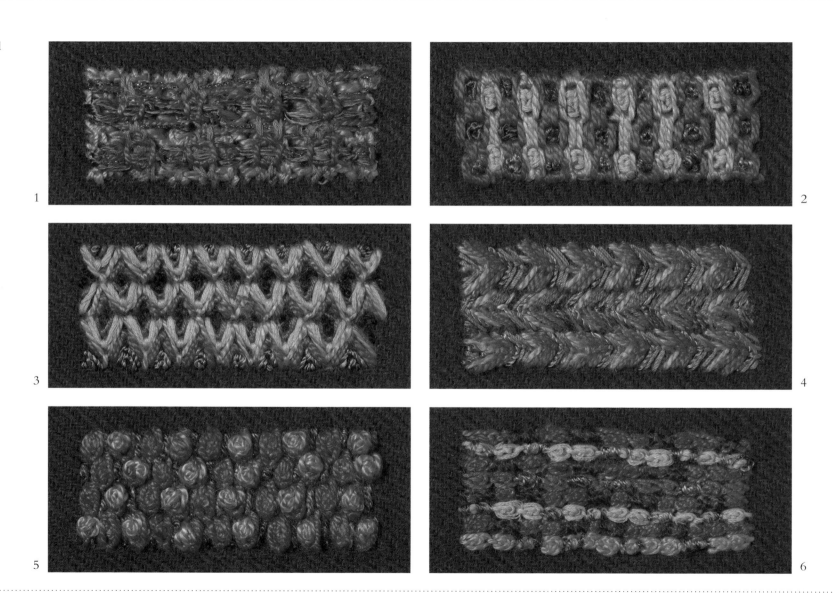

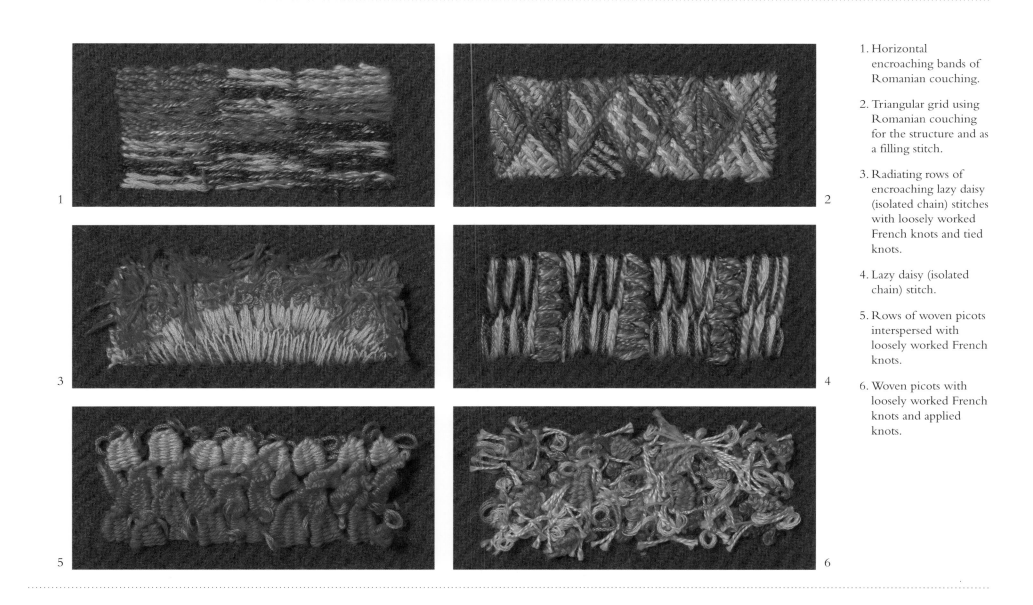

1. Horizontal encroaching bands of Romanian couching.

2. Triangular grid using Romanian couching for the structure and as a filling stitch.

3. Radiating rows of encroaching lazy daisy (isolated chain) stitches with loosely worked French knots and tied knots.

4. Lazy daisy (isolated chain) stitch.

5. Rows of woven picots interspersed with loosely worked French knots.

6. Woven picots with loosely worked French knots and applied knots.

Stitch Samples

1a. Raised chain band stitch worked haphazardly, overlapping and layered. Thin to thick yarns were used with additional beads.

1b. The stitch worked as a detached one varying the quality and scale of the yarns.

1c. Worked traditionally as a line stitch in a variety of threads some of which have been layered one of top of another and others wrapped with metallic filaments to highlight.

2a. Large silk French knots have been arranged in a circular pattern. Smaller ones have been stitched on top and medium sized stitches clustered around the main shapes. Bugle and round beads have been added to highlight.

2b. Tiny to large knots stitched closely together worked in a range of textured yarns. Some stitches have not been totally formed allowing small loops to protrude adding interest to the surface.

2c. These knots have been made by the final part of the stitch being stitched away from the main knot forming a 'leg'. Tiny beads stitched on the knots and vertically stitched bugle beads decorate the sample.

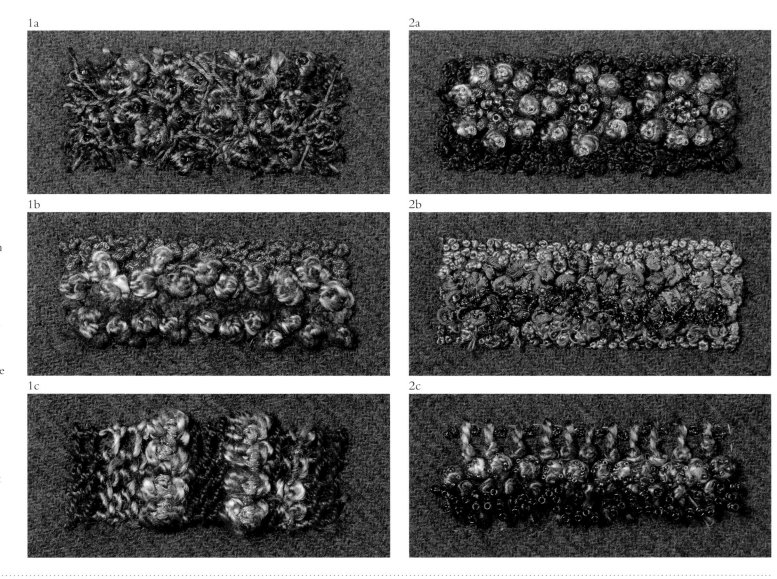

1a

2a

1b

2b

1c

2c

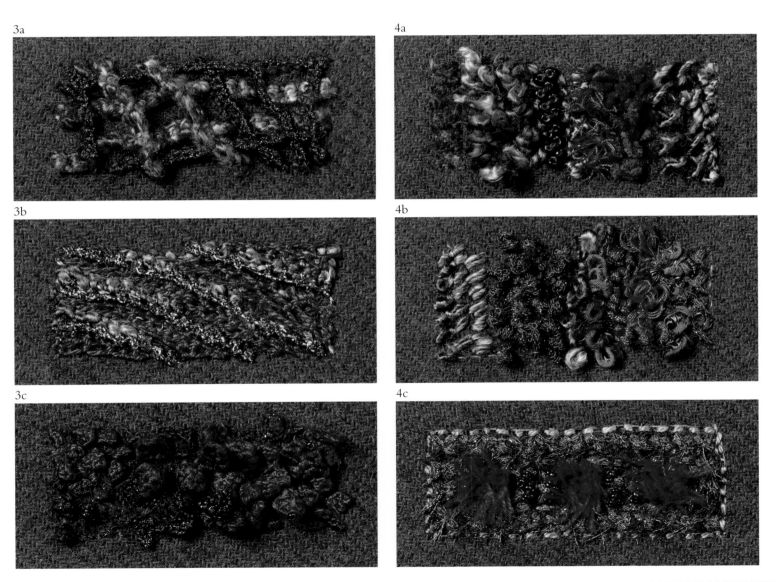

3a

4a

3b

4b

3c

4c

3a. The first shows lines of knotted buttonhole stitch worked on top of base one to create a dimensional grid effect.

3b. The same stitch worked more loosely giving a lacy look. Metallic crochet yarn provided a contrast to the cotton and silk threads.

3c. Buttonhole picots can be most effective when creating particular textural surfaces where protrusions are relevant. Rows of stitches are worked over straight stitch bars and not the ground cloth and on each return journey the stitch is worked in the previous one decreasing a stitch on each line.

4a. Velvet stitch usually selected for canvas work can be a useful and attractive one suitable for surface stitching. Selecting thick and thin yarns can give a totally different look.

4b. Knitting and weaving yarns exhibit novelty characteristics and can provide a range of effects. The dimensional loops can hold their shape or softly drape.

4c. All samples show some loops cut and beads incorporated.

Useful Information

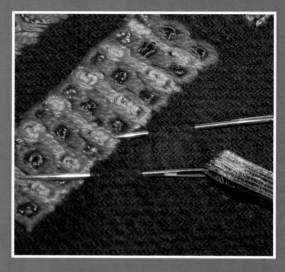

Hand stitching is so much more satisfying on backgrounds that accepts the needle and threads with ease. Soft wool and open weaves in linen or cotton can be very useful. The fabric pictured is an open weave cotton, dyed with washing machine dyes.

Cotton scrim is a wonderful soft fabric, really useful for incorporating into many types of work including embellishing with a needle punch machine and chopped up into textural grounds. It accepts dyes very easily and is an excellent material to have in your stock.

Needles are very important and often overlooked. They have many different functions and selecting the appropriate needle for the task can make stitching so much more satisfying. One of the functions of a needle is to ease the path of the thread through the fabric. The chenille needles pictured here are excellent for the chunky threads that form the basis of so much of our hand stitching. They have a sharp point and a large eye and the chenille 14 is a particularly useful one.

Transfer Foils come in many different types from gold and silver through to rainbow, iridescent and specialised patterns. They are very useful for creating backgrounds for stitch where a glistening hint may shine through, as well as for more obvious metallic textures. They are used in combination with specialised glues or 'Bondaweb'.

'Sculptafoam' and 'PenScore' or similar blocks respond to heat. Place silicone paper over the surface and iron to heat before removing the silicone and press in the dimensional item to be impressed. Wooden blocks work well and have the advantage of offering the opportunity of positive and negative images. Natural forms may also be used to make patterns in this useful material.

Stretching the work – Having worked stitching by hand or machine in a hoop or frame, many people do not think it necessary to damp stretch the piece when it is finished. However it makes such a difference to the professional look of the finished work that it is really worthwhile to put in the extra effort. On a soft board such as cork place dampened towel or paper towel and pin the work face upwards using dressmaking pins. Start in the middles and work outwards pulling firmly throughout. Leave to dry naturally and be amazed at how much better it looks. Be careful with fabrics such as silk if the dampness might affect the fabric. If the work is very distorted or puckered the reverse can be sprayed directly with water as a last resort, then pinned out as before, but only in emergencies.

It is important to be comfortable with the frames you select for both hand and machine embroidery. The selection illustrated show the conventional round frame with a screw to tighten the fabric within so making the material taut and suitable for free drawing on the machine. It is a good idea to tape the inside ring for extra grip. The rounded edged square frame is also extremely useful but is not readily available. The plastic frames ('EasyStreetCrafts' hoop frames) seen in the foreground are made in various shapes and sizes and are intended for small hand stitched pieces. They are light to handle, economical and very easy to use. The fabric is trapped tautly between the top and bottom of the frame so no tacks, pins or staples are required.

It is important to know the functions of various machine needles. They range from very fine ones for using with delicate fabrics to others that can be selected for stretchy materials or tough denim.
However, topstitch needles sized 90–120 are good for free motion machine work when using a wide range of machine threads. They have a much larger eye and deeper groove running down the shank of the needle which enables the threads to run through smoothly so lessening the problem of thread breakage. Other needles have been designed specifically for metallic and Lana yarns. Needles need to be changed quite frequently as blunt ones can cause missed stitches.

Sketchbooks come in all sorts of shapes and sizes. The ones shown have all appeared from time to time in a number of Double Trouble Enterprises publications. They contain paper that can endure paint without puckering the surface as well as the weight of additional collage. The differing shapes, proportions and formats can help encourage images to be developed in a less obvious way.

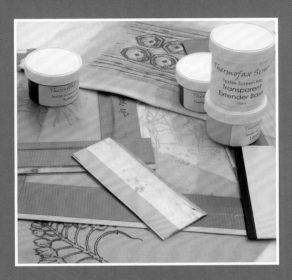  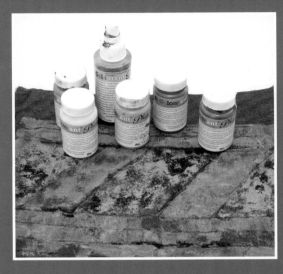

Thermofax Screens have also made transferring a design onto material a much easier process. An image can be drawn with a bold line, photocopied and sent to an appropriate supplier in order to make the screen. They can be used to create a one off image, printing haphazard arrangements all over the fabric or in formal repeating units. Nearly all fabrics are suitable and the printed image when dry can be heat set with a dry iron. Many fabric paints are suitable but washing out the screens at the end of printing is essential so that they can be used again.

Tap paper or Jet FX, an artists transfer paper is very useful for transferring designs onto cloth. You can print, draw, crayon or paint an image on to the paper which can then be transferred by iron on to most types of fabric. Some designs may have to be drawn in reverse as a mirror image.

'deColourant Plus' is a comparatively new product in this form and has been devised to make the technique of discharging colour from a cloth much easier. When applied to a dyed fabric it puts a new colour in while taking the base colour out. When dry, ironing the material using a steam iron completes the action. Previously, the discharge paste was mixed with colour and the proportions of which were not always foolproof.

Pattern Pathways – On Reflection

Looking back, looking forward

We continue to emphasise the importance of focussed observation and all the stitched samples in this book have a tangible source based on objects or places that had an attraction. The added factor was that we were looking specifically for patterns and rhythms so in each case there was a purposeful journey that lead from initial idea through design exploration to a finished piece. There are many techniques for developing imagery and we hope that some of those used will lead you onto your own pattern pathway.

We both enjoy responding to challenges that encourage us to break boundaries and explore new materials and methods but the most important factor in developing ideas is to find a source of inspiration that really engages you and that can develop into a passionate involvement that generates it's own momentum. There are many UFOs (unfinished objects) languishing in cupboards but if the idea had been really exciting it would probably have been finished. Sometimes a prolonged break during the working period will result in a lack of impetus and that can also be a reason not to complete work.

Looking back

When embarking on new work it can be useful to review previous work and select the pieces that still hold intrigue or potential. It is all too easy to forget useful techniques and working methods so an ongoing workbook is useful. It is also a temptation to keep treading a familiar pathway. A notice board can be helpful when selecting working pathways, providing it is kept current and relevant not just decoration. Finding worthwhile areas for work usually involves a continual process of selection and elimination.

Consolidating

From the most promising of previous work develop further explorative samples from which to select and so on until a real sense of excitement grows. Continue to update your notice board to stress the focus.

Looking forward

The desire to begin stitching can be compelling so the single stitch examples that we have included could satisfy that need. However, working in a series so that each one leads to another will really pay dividends. Sometimes, working on just one piece can be frustrating but planning several means that ideas can be better worked through and problems resolved on the next piece. Not all of them will work but the most successful can be selected. It is a hard lesson to learn but not all work succeeds equally and when working 'one offs' it is not always possible to analyse, evaluate, benefit and move on to better results.

There are no short cuts to producing satisfying work but we honestly believe that by working through the processes detailed here it is possible to work in a more focussed and worthwhile manner and provide you with the impetus to work in a more rewarding way.

Opposite: Design derived from sketchbook on pages 78–79. Techniques include applied shapes in a soluble sandwich in preparation for machine embroidery. Actual size.

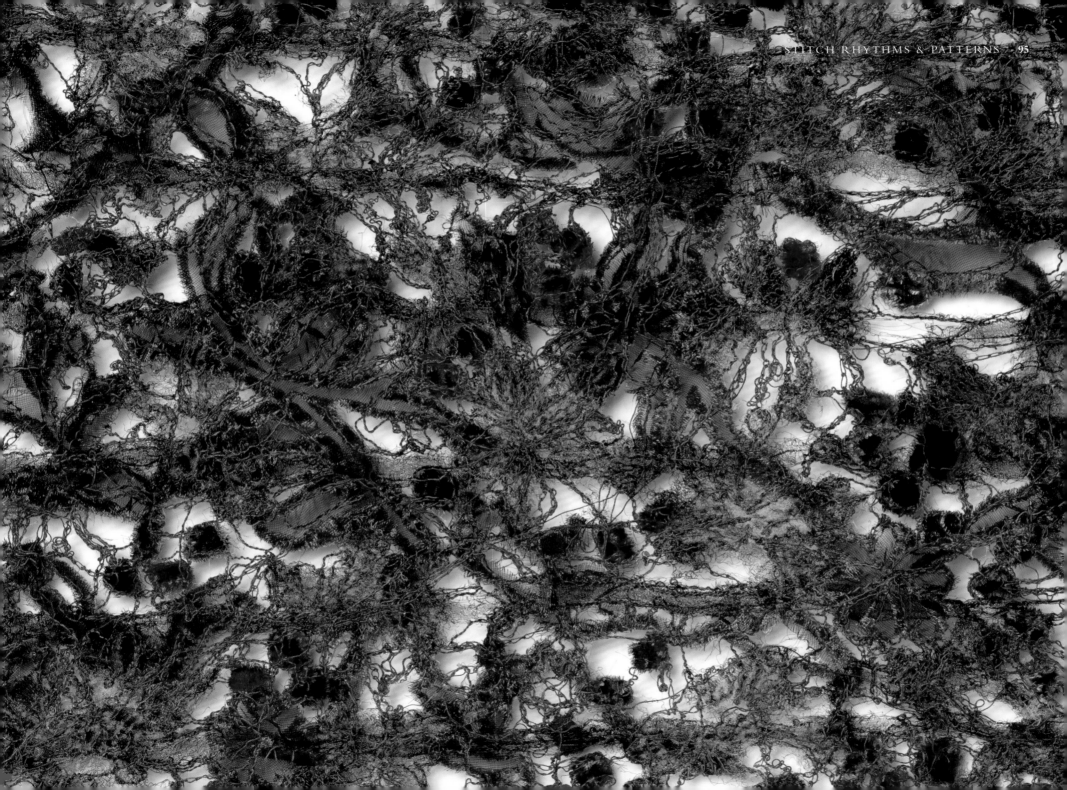

Acknowledgements

Our greatest thanks as ever go to our husbands, Philip Littlejohn and Steve Udall who support us in every way. We would also like to thank Michael Wicks, our photographer and book designer Jason Horsburgh for their professional contributions.

All photography was by Michael with the exception of location shots by the authors and their husbands.

Suggestions

Visit all types of exhibitions and read about other artists, their styles and motivation.

Information

For information on suppliers, events and future book releases visit our website. There are also books and DVDs available to order online.

www.doubletrouble-ent.com

DVDs Available

Jan Beaney
Jean Littlejohn
Seeing Double
In Action

Visit our website for information on suppliers, events and other books available. www.doubletrouble -ent.com

Further Reading

For a full list of books available and future releases visit www.doubletrouble-ent.com

Stitchscapes – ISBN: 978-9559959-4-1

Original Series

Book no: Title:
1. Vanishing Act
2. Voluptuous Velvet
3. Bonding & Beyond
4. Transfer to Transform
5. Gardens & More
6. Conversations with Constance
7. Trees as a Theme
8. Giving Pleasure
9. New Dimensions
10. Double Vision
11. A Tale of Two Stitches
12. A Sketch in Time
13. No Stone Unturned
14. Connections
15. Colour Explorations
16. Over the Line
17. Grids to Stitch
18. Seductive Surfaces
19. RED
20. Embellish & Enrich
21. Location, Location
22. Seeing Double
23. Fragile Fabrics
24. Constructions

© copyright – Jan Beaney & Jean Littlejohn 2011

First published October 2011

Published by:
Double Trouble Enterprises
PO Box 348
Maidenhead
Berkshire
SL6 6XB
Fax: +44(0) 1628 675699
www.doubletrouble-ent.com

ISBN: 978-0-9559959-5-8

Designed by Jason Horsburgh.
Printed by Gemini Press Ltd.